NUTCASES

CONSTITUTIONAL AND ADMINISTRATIVE LAW

AUSTRALIA
LBC Information Services
Sydney

CANADA and USA
Carswell
Toronto · Ontario

NEW ZEALAND
Brooker's
Auckland

SINGAPORE and MALAYSIA
Thomson Information (S.E. Asia)
Singapore

NUTCASES

CONSTITUTIONAL AND ADMINISTRATIVE LAW

FIRST EDITION

by

MAUREEN SPENCER
BA, LLM
Senior Lecturer in Law
Middlesex University

JOHN SPENCER
MA, LLM
Barrister

London · Hong Kong · Dublin
Sweet & Maxwell
1997

Published in 1997 by
Sweet & Maxwell Limited
of 100 Avenue Road
London, NW3 3PF
(http://www.smlawpub.co.uk)

Reprinted 1999

Phototypeset by J&L Composition Ltd, Filey, North Yorkshire
Printed in England by Clays Ltd., St Ives plc

No natural forests were destroyed to make this product:
only farmed timber was used and re-planted

ISBN 0 421 604301

**A CIP catalogue record for this book is available
from the British Library**

CONTENTS

TABLE OF CASES

TABLE OF STATUTES

1. GENERAL PRINCIPLES OF THE CONSTITUTION

Role of Conventions

KEY PRINCIPLE: *Conventions may be recognised by the courts but are not enforced by them.*

Madzimbamuto v. Lardner-Burke

A state of emergency was proclaimed in the Crown colony of Southern Rhodesia on November 5, 1965 and the following day the Justice and Law and Order Minister ordered the detention of a number of people including the plaintiff's husband. On November 11, the Southern Rhodesian Prime Minister unilaterally declared independence. The colony's governor issued a proclamation on behalf of the Queen that the government ceased to hold office and called on all citizens to refrain from acts which would further the objectives of the illegal authorities. On November 16, Parliament passed the Southern Rhodesia Act which provided that no laws could be made or business transacted by the Rhodesian legislative assembly. In February 1966 the state of emergency was illegally renewed and the Justice and Law and Order Minister made an order under it renewing the detention of the plaintiff's husband. She challenged in the courts the legality of her husband's detention.

HELD: (PC) The emergency powers regulations made after November 11, 1965 had no legal validity, force or effect and the detention order made under them was invalid. While the legitimate government was trying to regain control it was impossible to hold that the usurping government was for any purpose a lawful government. Even if there was a principle which recognised the need to preserve law and order in territory controlled by a usurper, such a principle could not override the legal right of the U.K. Parliament to legislate for a territory under the sovereignty of the Queen in the U.K. Parliament. The appeal was allowed. [1969] 1 A.C. 645

COMMENTARY

In passing the Southern Rhodesia Act 1965 Parliament was ignoring the previous constitutional convention that it would not exercise its sovereignty in Commonwealth affairs without the consent of the Rhodesian government. In giving judgment Lord Reid said:

> "It is often said that it would be unconstitutional for the United Kingdom Parliament to do certain things, meaning that the moral, political and other reasons against doing them are so strong that most people would regard it as highly improper if Parliament did these things. . . . It may be that it would have been thought, before 1965, that it would be unconstitutional to disregard this convention. But it may also be that the unilateral Declaration of Independence released the United Kingdom from any obligation to observe the convention. Their Lordships in declaring the law are not concerned with these matters. They are only concerned with the legal powers of Parliament."

KEY PRINCIPLE: *The conventional doctrine of Cabinet secrecy can give rise to a duty of confidentiality enforceable in equity.*

Attorney-General v. Jonathan Cape

Richard Crossman, a Cabinet minister, kept a political diary and after his death the diary was sent to the Cabinet Secretary for approval before publication. The Cabinet Secretary refused to authorise publication, and the literary executors undertook not to publish without prior notice to the Treasury Solicitor. When extracts began to be published in *The Sunday Times*, the Attorney-General sought an injunction against further publication.

HELD: (QB) The court had power to restrain publication of information in breach of confidence. Cabinet discussions were confidential until such time as their disclosure would not undermine the doctrine of joint Cabinet responsibility. But that given the lapse of time since the discussions from 1964-66 the contents of the diary would not undermine the doctrine, so there were no grounds for granting an injunction. [1976] Q.B. 752

COMMENTARY

The court came close here to enforcing a convention. In an appropriate case the court would, it appears, intervene to uphold by injunction the maintenance of the doctrine of Cabinet confidentiality since this was in the public interest.

KEY PRINCIPLE: *Conventions can only become laws by statutory intervention.*

Reference Re Amendment of the Constitution of Canada

The government of Quebec referred certain questions to the provincial Court of Appeal including the following:"Does the Canadian constitution empower, whether by statute, convention or otherwise, the Senate and the House of Commons of Canada to cause the constitution to be amended without the consent of the provinces and in spite of the objection of several of them, in such a manner as to affect (i) the legislative competence of the provincial legislatures in virtue of the Canadian constitution? (ii) the status or role of the provincial legislatures or governments within the Canadian federation?" The matter went on appeal to the Supreme Court of Canada.

HELD: (Supreme Court) A majority of the court held that as a matter of convention the constitution did not so empower the Senate and House of Commons of Canada, but that as a matter of law it did. The majority held also that the nature of a convention was inconsistent with its legal enforcement. (1982) 125 D.L.R. (3d) 1

COMMENTARY
The judgment gives a very succinct summary of the differences between laws and conventions.

"The main purpose of constitutional conventions is to ensure that the legal framework of the constitution will be operated in accordance with the prevailing constitutional values or principles of the period . . . Perhaps the main reason why conventional rules cannot be enforced by the Courts is that they are generally in conflict with the legal rules which they postulate and the Courts are bound to enforce the legal rules. The conflict is not of a type which would entail the commission of any illegality. It results from the fact that legal rules create wide powers, discretions and rights which conventions prescribe should be exercised only in a certain limited manner, if at all."

Rule of Law

KEY PRINCIPLE: *The executive cannot lawfully assume powers which are not known to the courts.*

Entick v. Carrington

Two King's messengers, acting under a warrant issued by the Secretary of State, broke into the plaintiff's house and carried off his papers. The action was part of an investigation into certain seditious articles. The plaintiff sued the messengers for trespass. They claimed to have acted lawfully under the Secretary of State's warrant.

HELD: The warrant was illegal and without effect. The Secretary of State could invade the rights of a subject only if his action was authorised by law. No statute or common law right authorised the invasion of the plaintiff's house. The argument of the Secretary of State that the power to issue such a warrant was essential to government had no validity. (1765) 19 St. Tr. 1029

KEY PRINCIPLE: *The state does not need express authority for its actions if they do not breach common law or statute.*

Malone v. Metropolitan Police Commissioner (No. 2)

The plaintiff was charged with handling stolen goods. At his trial, the prosecution admitted that his telephone had been tapped under a warrant from the Home Secretary and his conversations recorded. He brought proceedings against the Home Secretary for a declaration that the phone tapping was unlawful.

HELD: (Ch D) The tapping of a telephone could lawfully be done because there was nothing to make it unlawful. No statute authorised phone tapping with or without a warrant. But that did not mean tapping was unlawful. A search of premises which was not authorised by law was illegal because it involved the tort of trespass. But no act of trespass was involved in telephone tapping. [1979] Ch. 344

COMMENTARY
The case may be contrasted with *Entick v. Carrington*. In that case the state needed express authority which it did not have because the search warrant was expressed in general terms. Without express authority it was committing the tort of trespass. There is no tort of the invasion of privacy and so the

Post Office did not need express authority for the tapping of telephones at the request of the police.

KEY PRINCIPLE: *The common law is the guardian of rights of the individual.*

Derbyshire County Council v. The Times Newspapers

A local authority brought a libel action against a newspaper which had questioned the propriety of its handling of a super-annuation fund. On a preliminary point, the judge held that the council could sue for libel in respect of its governmental and administrative functions. That decision was reversed in the Court of Appeal and the council appealed.

HELD: (HL) Uninhibited public criticism of an elected body was vital in a democracy. The threat of libel actions would inhibit legitimate criticism. It was contrary to the public interest for central or local government institutions to have any common law right to sue for libel. The action would be struck out. [1993] A.C. 534

COMMENTARY

The Court of Appeal applied Article 10 of the European Convention of Human Rights in finding that a local authority cannot sue for libel. The House of Lords however held that in this case the common law could determine the issue in favour of protecting free speech. *Per* Lord Keith "It is of the highest public importance that a democratically elected governmental body . . . should be open to uninhibited public criticism". The case is an important instance of a robust use of the common law to protect individual rights. The House acknowledged however the guidance of the Court of Appeal judgment in cases where the common law was uncertain.

KEY PRINCIPLE: *The executive is not above the law.*

M v. Home Office

A citizen of Zaire sought political asylum, which was refused, as was his application for leave to bring judicial review proceedings. A date was set for his removal and on that day, shortly before he was due to be removed, he made a renewed application in the Court of Appeal for leave to move. The judge understood counsel for the Home Secretary to have given an undertaking that the removal would not go ahead while the application was being considered. However his removal went ahead. When the judge heard that he had been removed, he ordered the Secretary of State to organise his return to the jurisdiction. Home Office officials took steps to comply with the judge's order, but they were overruled by the Secretary of State in reliance on legal advice that the order had been made without jurisdiction, being a mandatory interim injunction against an officer of the Crown. The judge dismissed a motion for committal, but it was allowed in part by the Court of Appeal. Both parties appealed.

HELD: (HL) The Secretary of State had not been entitled to claim Crown immunity, since an action could be brought against him personally for a tort committed or authorised by him in his official capacity, and an injunction could be granted against him in that capacity. The Crown itself could not be found in contempt, but a government department or a minister could. The injunction had been granted against the Secretary of State in his official capacity, and the department for which he was responsible was in contempt. Accordingly, the appropriate finding was that the Secretary of State for the Home Department was in contempt. [1994] 1 A.C. 377

COMMENTARY

Lord Templeman put the decision in a historical context. ". . . the argument that there is no power to enforce the law by injunction or contempt proceedings against a minister in his official capacity would, if upheld, establish the proposition that the executive obey the law as a matter of grace and not as a matter of necessity, a proposition which would reverse the result of the Civil War".

It was held however that since the Home Secretary had acted on advice it would not be proper to find him personally in contempt of court.

Doctrine of Separation of Powers

KEY PRINCIPLE: *The judiciary's task is to apply legislation and not interpret it such a way as to provide their own view of what the law should be.*

Duport Steels Ltd v. Sirs

The government used its statutory powers to stop public invest-
ment in the British Steel Corporation, obliging it to meet
operating costs out of earnings. As a consequence pay negotiations broke down and the Iron and Steel Trades Confederation
called a strike in the Corporation, which was a nationalised
industry. Two weeks into the strike, the union called out its
members in the private steel companies as a way of putting
pressure on the government. Sixteen private steel companies
sought an injunction against the ISTC. The judge refused, but
the Court of Appeal granted, the injunction on the basis that
the ISTC was really in dispute with the government, not the
employers, and the economic consequences were so disastrous
that the extension of the strike should be prevented. The union
appealed.

HELD: (HL) Provided a person honestly believed he was
acting in the course or furtherance of an industrial dispute,
he was entitled to immunity in tort. The court was not entitled
to look at the remoteness of the act from the immediate source
of the dispute, or the extent to which it had reasonable pro-
spects of furthering the dispute, save in assessing the genuine-
ness of the defendants' professed purpose. Parliament might
not have expected when it granted the relevant immunities that
they would be used so as to produce consequences so injurious
to the nation. But the legal limit on those immunities was set by
the construction of the statute, not by judges making their own
preferred amendments where they felt necessary in the public
interest. [1980] 1 W.L.R. 142

COMMENTARY

Here the relationship between the courts and Parliament is
set out. The judges have a great deal of discretionary power,
as Lord Scarman said "to do justice so wide that they may
be regarded as law makers". Lord Diplock said in the course
of his judgment: "at a time when more and more cases
involve the application of legislation which gives effect to
policies that are the subject of bitter public and parliamentary
controversy, it cannot be too strongly emphasised that the
British constitution, though largely unwritten, is firmly based
upon the separation of powers: Parliament makes the laws,
the judiciary interpret them."

KEY PRINCIPLE: *The United Kingdom has Treaty obligations to change the law so as to comply with human rights obligations under the European Convention of Human Rights.*

The Sunday Times v. The United Kingdom

The Sunday Times brought an action before the European Commission on Human Rights claiming that the injunction upheld by the House of Lords [1974] A.C. 273 infringed their right to freedom of expression guaranteed by Article 10 of the European Convention on Human Rights. The Commission referred the case to the Court of Human Rights.

HELD: (ECHR) The interference with the applicants' freedom of expression was not justified under Article 10(2) which permitted such restrictions "as are prescribed by law and are necessary in a democratic society . . . for maintaining the authority and impartiality of the judiciary". There was no "pressing social need" for the injunction. [1979] 2 E.H.R.R. 245

COMMENTARY
This is one example where the United Kingdom has introduced legislation to implement the Court of Human Rights' decisions. The judgment led to the Contempt of Court Act 1981. The Convention has not yet been incorporated into English law so any obligation on the United Kingdom derives from international law. Decisions of the Court can result from two procedures, either individual petition or (more rarely) one state taking action against another. The Convention allows states to derogate from obligations as the United Kingdom did in relation to the finding in *Brogan v. United Kingdom* (1988) 11 E.H.R.R. 117. The power of detention under what is now the Prevention of Terrorism(Temporary) Provisions Act 1989, s.14 was held to breach Article 6, the right to a fair trial by a impartial tribunal.

KEY PRINCIPLE: *The European Convention on Human Rights does not place a limit on the exercise of statutory discretion.*

R. v. Secretary of State for Home Department, ex p. Brind

The Secretary of State made orders under the Broadcasting Act 1981 banning television and radio stations from broad-

casting the words spoken by spokesmen of organisations proscribed under anti-terrorism legislation. Broadcasters sought
judicial review of the orders as being outside the Secretary of
State's powers because the ban was disproportionate to its
ostensible object of preventing intimidation by the organisations concerned and also because he should have regard to the
European Convention on Human Rights. The application was
dismissed by the Divisional Court and by the Court of Appeal.
The broadcasters appealed.

HELD: (HL) Where there is no ambiguity the European Convention need not be applied. [1991] 1 A.C. 696

COMMENTARY
Lord Ackner said that since there was no ambiguity in the
relevant section of the statute there was here no need to have
recourse to the Convention. He said that the limits placed
upon discretion were that the power should be used for the
purpose for which it was granted and that it must be exercised
reasonably in the Wednesbury sense. He also referred to
Lord Denning's judgement in *R. v. Chief Immigration Officer,
ex p. Salamat Bibi* [1976] 1 W.L.R. 979 where he said:

  "The position as I understand it is that if there is any ambiguity in our statutes, or uncertainty in our law, then these
  courts can look to the Convention as an aid to clear up the
  ambiguity and uncertainty".

---

2. PARLIAMENTARY SUPREMACY

KEY PRINCIPLE: *An Act of Parliament takes precedence
over international law.*

Mortensen v. Peters 1906
The captain of a Norwegian trawler was convicted of fishing
with an otter trawl net in the Moray Firth contrary to the
Herring Fishery (Scotland) Act 1889. He appealed on the
grounds that he was not a British subject and had not been
fishing in territorial waters.

HELD: (Court of Session) If the captain's conduct fell within
the Act , the court was bound to give effect to its terms. There

was a presumption that parliament would not seek to exceed what an international tribunal might hold to be its proper sphere of legislative competence. However, that presumption had been overtaken by the plain words of the statute. (1906) 8 F.(J.) 93

COMMENTARY

The courts have here and in other cases acknowledged a presumption that Parliament would not seek to exceed what an international tribunal might hold to be its proper sphere of legislative competence but the presumption would fall in the face of express statutory words or clear implication. The standing of international treaties is important in assessing the status of the European Convention on Human Rights (see page 8).

KEY PRINCIPLE: *The monarch cannot add to or amend legislation or the common law by means of a proclamation.*

Case of Proclamations

James I was short of money and issued a proclamation declaring it to be against the law to build new houses in London or to make wheat starch. His aim was to levy fines from offenders.

HELD: (Court of Common Pleas) The king could not by proclamation change the common law or create any new offences. The king had no prerogative powers other than those allowed by the law. However, if he proclaimed an existing offence that offence would in future be aggravated. (1611) 12 Co. Rep. 74

COMMENTARY

The Bill of Rights 1688 confirmed that it would be illegal for the monarch to attempt without the approval of Parliament to impose taxes, suspend the operation of laws, or dispense with penalties. Earlier, in *Dr Bonham's Case*, (1610) 8 Co. Rep. 114 the court had referred to a higher natural or fundamental law which not even an Act of Parliament could override but this doctrine has not been of practical importance since the English Revolution (see page 11).

KEY PRINCIPLE: *Courts have no power to challenge the validity of an Act of Parliament.*

R. v. Jordan

The leader of a right-wing party was imprisoned for 18 months for offences against the Race Relations Act 1965. He sought legal aid to bring an action for habeas corpus on the ground that his rights of free speech had been unlawfully curtailed by the Act, which was consequently invalid.

HELD: The courts had no power to question the validity of an Act of Parliament, which was supreme. [1967] Crim. L.R. 483

COMMENTARY

One often debated issue is whether the common law could strike out an Act of Parliament as repugnant to natural justice. In *Dr Bonham's Case* the president censors of the College of Physicians ordered the plaintiff to be committed to prison because he had continued to practice medicine when ordered not to do so and refused to pay fines levied for having done so. The plaintiff claimed to practice under a degree awarded by Cambridge University. He brought an action against the president and censors of the college for false imprisonment. It was held that the censors had no power to commit the plaintiff to prison, since their power was limited to the control of bad practice and not of good practice of medicine. The order for the plaintiff's imprisonment had been wrongly made by the president and censors of the college, though only the censors had jurisdiction even in cases of bad practice. The college should have given written rather than oral reasons for their decision. Lord Coke C.J. said:

> "And it appears in our books, that in many cases, the common law will control Acts of Parliament and sometimes adjudge them to be utterly void: for when an Act of Parliament is against common right and reason or repugnant or impossible to be performed, the common law will control it and adjudge such an Act to be void".

The problem has not been a live issue since then.

KEY PRINCIPLE: *It is for Parliament not the courts to investigate whether an Act had been obtained in breach of Parliamentary procedure.*

British Railways Board v. Pickin

A railway line was constructed under an Act of 1836 by which the lands on which it was built should, if abandoned, revert to the owner of the adjoining lands. The lands were subsequently vested in the British Railways Board. In 1968 the Board obtained a private Act of Parliament, the British Railways Act, which nullified the effect of the 1836 Act and vested abandoned lands in the Board. The plaintiff owned land beside the track and claimed to own the track to its centre-line. He said the Board had misled Parliament by a false preamble to the 1968 Act, and in obtaining the unopposed passage of the Bill. The judge struck out those sections of the plaintiff's claim, but they were reinstated in the Court of Appeal. The Board appealed.

HELD: (HL) The court's function was to consider and apply Acts of Parliament. It was not open to a litigant to impugn the validity of statute by seeking to establish that Parliament had been misled. Nor if Parliament had been misled, would that enable a litigant to establish a claim in equity against the other party. The court would not look into the manner in which Parliament had exercised its function. [1974] A.C. 765

COMMENTARY

This principle is known as the enrolled act rule. The courts cannot question the procedure by which an Act of Parliament is passed any more than its content. The following case appeared to suggest that this principle may not always apply.

Manuel v. Attorney-General

The Queen gave royal assent to the Canada Act 1982 which authorised a new procedure for amending the Canadian constitution, in which the U.K. Parliament would no longer have any part. The legislation recognised and affirmed the existing aboriginal and treaty rights of the Indian peoples of Canada. A number of Indian chiefs, representing their peoples, issued writs against the Attorney-General seeking declarations that the U.K. Parliament had no power to amend the Canadian constitution so as to prejudice the Indian nations without their consent and that the Canada Act 1982 was *ultra vires* because it was inconsistent with the constitutional safeguards provided for the Indian peoples in the Statute of Westminster 1931. The Attorney-General moved to have the chiefs' applications struck out as showing no cause of action. The judge held that the Canada Act 1982 was not *ultra vires* and that he had a duty to apply it, and that the Attorney-General was the wrong defendant, since the obligations the chiefs sought to enforce were those of the Queen in right of Canada, and not the Crown in right of the United Kingdom. The chiefs appealed.

HELD: (CA) The only requirement imposed by the Statute of Westminster (a certificate to which Canada had requested the change) had been complied with, so that even if the Canada Act 1982 had to comply with the Statute of Westminster, it had done so. The applications had been correctly struck out. [1983] 1 Ch. 77

COMMENTARY
Megarry V.C. in the Chancery Division had held that the case was covered by *British Railways Board v. Pickin.* The Court of Appeal however accepted that prior consent of the Dominion of Canada might have been required to make a valid Act but that in this case the preamble to the statute declared on its face that it had such consent.

Doctrine of Implied Repeal

KEY PRINCIPLE: *The provisions of a later Act in so far as they are inconsistent with those of an earlier Act must prevail. Parliament cannot bind itself as to the substance or the form of subsequent legislation.*

Ellen Street Estates Ltd v. Minister of Health
Section 7 of the Acquisition of Land (Assessment of Compensation) Act 1919 enacted that the provisions of the Act or order by which land was authorised to be acquired, or of any Act incorporated therewith "Shall in relation to the matters dealt with in this Act, have effect subject to this Act, and in so far as inconsistent with this Act those provisions shall cease to have or shall not have effect." An improvement scheme was made in 1922 over an area of the East End of London, part of which was owned by the plaintiff. The scheme lapsed without being acted on, but was subsequently revived by the London County Council under the Housing Act 1925. The plaintiff claimed

that the 1925 Act was inconsistent with section 7 of the 1919 Act. The judge upheld the revived scheme and the plaintiff appealed.

HELD: (CA) Parliament could not bind itself as to the form of subsequent legislation. It was impossible for Parliament to enact that in a subsequent statute dealing with the same subject-matter there could be no implied repeal. Where a subsequent Act of Parliament indicated that the earlier statute was being to some extent repealed, the court must give effect to that intention. [1934] 1 K.B. 590

COMMENTARY

In *Manuel v. Attorney-General* (see above at page 12) the Court accepted that its proposition that the Statute of Westminster could restrict the form of subsequent legislation in requiring Dominion consent to constitutional change was in conflict with *Ellen Street Estates Ltd v. Minister of Health*. But it said it was not pronouncing on the matter. The orthodox doctrine of implied repeal has however been modified by the European Communities Act (see below at page 17) and by authorities from subordinate legislatures.

KEY PRINCIPLE: *A Bill from a subordinate legislature cannot become law in violation of a constitutional requirement.*

Attorney-General for New South Wales v. Trethowan

The New South Wales legislature in 1929 amended the Constitution Act 1902 to provide by section 7A that no Bill for abolishing the legislative council should be presented for the royal assent until it had been approved by a referendum of electors. The same was to apply to a Bill for repealing section 7A. The following year both Houses of the legislature passed Bills abolishing the legislative council and repealing section 7A. Two members of the legislative council sued the state Attorney-General for a declaration that the Bills could not lawfully be presented for Royal Assent until approved by the electors in accordance with section 7A. The matter came by way of appeal to the Privy Council.

HELD: (PC) The provision that Bills must be approved by the electors before being presented was a provision as to "manner

and form" under section 5 of the Colonial Laws Validity Act
1865 which empowered the state legislature to make laws
respecting the constitution, powers and procedure of the legislature. Section 5 provided that legislation comply with such
provisions as to manner and form as might from time to time
be required by Act of Parliament, letters patent, Order in
Council or colonial law. Accordingly, the Bills could not lawfully
be presented until they had been approved by a majority of the
electors voting. [1932] A.C. 526

Bribery Commissioner v. Ranasinghe

The respondent had been tried before a Bribery Commission
on a charge of bribery and challenged orders made against him
on the grounds that the persons composing the tribunal were
not validly appointed, since they had been appointed under the
Bribery Amendment Act 1958. That Act provided that the
tribunal members be appointed by the Governor-General on
the advice of the Justice Minister. It conflicted with the Ceylon
(Constitution) Order in Council 1946 which provided by section 55 that "the appointment . . . of judicial officers is hereby
vested in the Judicial Service Commission."

HELD: (PC) The Ceylon legislature had no power to ignore
conditions of law-making imposed by the instrument which
itself regulated the power to make law. This was so even where
the legislature was sovereign, as was the Ceylon legislature. The
constitution could be amended or altered by the legislature if
the regulating instrument so provided and if its terms were
complied with, but the mere fact of the establishment of a
legislature did not give it some inherent power to overrule
the provisions of the instrument by which it was established.
The court accepted that an alternative, narrower, view was
taken in regard to English law. However, it pointed out there
was never a need for U.K. courts to look into the process of a
Bill becoming law because there was no governing instrument
which prescribed law making powers. [1965] A.C. 172

COMMENTARY

It appears that these cases contradict *British Railways Board
v. Pickin* (see above at page 12). But their subject-matter is
proceedings in subordinate legislatures so they are not
authority for the practice of the Westminster Parliament.

KEY PRINCIPLE: *The Act of Union 1707 did not limit the power of the Westminster Parliament to legislate on public rights.*

MacCormick v. Lord Advocate

The petitioners objected to the Queen's being styled in Scotland as "Queen Elizabeth II". In the Outer House the petition was dismissed because the adoption of the numeral had been expressly authorised by the Royal Titles Act 1953, and an Act of Parliament could not be challenged in any court for breach of the Treaty of Union or any other cause. Further, the Treaty of Union did not expressly or by implication prohibit the use of the numeral and in any event the petitioners had no legal title or interests to sue. The petitioners appealed to the First Division.

HELD: The Royal Titles Act 1953 had no real bearing on the matter. The numeral "II" had been adopted on the Queen's accession in consequence of a practice of numbering sovereigns from the Norman conquest of England which the court would not criticise. However, the principle of unlimited parliamentary sovereignty had no counterpart in Scots law. The Scottish king and Parliament never acquired unlimited powers and so such powers could not have been transferred to the new Parliament of Great Britain in 1707. There was no provision in the union legislation that the Parliament of Great Britain should be absolutely sovereign. But the Court of Session was not competent to declare legislation as regards public law *ultra vires*. (1953) 69 L.Q.R. 512

Gibson v. Lord Advocate

The Act of Union 1707 allowed Parliament to change Scots law save that "no alteration be made in laws which concern private right except for evident utility of the subjects within Scotland". Relying on the Act, a Scottish fisherman challenged EEC regulations which opened Scottish waters to fishermen from other Member States.

HELD: (Court of Session) The court could not rule on whether a particular Act of the U.K. Parliament altering a particular aspect of Scots private law was or was not "for the evident utility" of the subjects within Scotland. It might be a different matter if Parliament proposed to abolish the Court of Session or the Church of Scotland or to substitute English law for the whole body of Scots private law. (1975) S.L.T. 134

COMMENTARY

When the Scottish and English Parliaments passed the Acts of Union they in effect declared their own abolition as separate organs and created a new sovereign entity, the British Parliament. Thus, in theory, Parliament could again limit its sovereignty by giving its sovereignty to another Parliament. This has led some to argue that Parliament has the ability to limit its legislative power. Some of the dicta in the above cases have appeared to indicate that the courts might in certain circumstances be prepared to question legislation which might be in violation of the Act of Union, specifically in relation to private rights. It is important to stress however that the attitude of the courts towards Parliamentary supremacy has always been essentially realistic and practical.

Impact of the European Community

The E.C.'s view—new legal order

KEY PRINCIPLE: *Member States permanently limited their sovereign rights by transferring powers from their domestic legal systems to the E.C. Community law prevails over domestic legal provisions.*

Costa v. ENEL

Italy nationalised electricity production and distribution and transferred the assets of private electricity companies to a new state body, ENEL. Costa, a shareholder in one of the private companies, claimed in an Italian court that the nationalisation infringed the Treaty of Rome. The magistrate requested a preliminary ruling under Article 177 of the Treaty.

HELD: (ECJ) Community law prevailed over incompatible national law, even where the national law had been enacted after the relevant Community law. The Member States had in certain spheres restricted their sovereign rights and created a body of law applicable both to their nationals and to themselves. (Case 6/64) [1964] E.C.R. 585, C.M.L.R. 425

COMMENTARY

The "new legal order" is both recognised in international law and also impacts on the domestic legal systems of Member States. Some rights and duties flowing from Community law have direct effect in the Member States meaning that they are directly enforceable in the national courts.

KEY PRINCIPLE: *European Communities Act, s. 2(1):*

"All such rights, powers, liabilities, obligations and restrictions from time to time created or arising by or under the Treaties, and all such remedies and procedures from time to time provided for by or under the Treaties, as in accordance with the Treaties are without further enactment to be given legal effect or used in the United Kingdom shall be recognised and available in law, and be enforced, allowed and followed accordingly, and the expression 'enforceable community right' and similar expressions shall be read as referring to one to which this subsection refers."

KEY PRINCIPLE: *Enforceable community rights including Article 119 of the EEC Treaty should be given effect in U.K. law.*

McCarthy's v. Smith

A woman warehouse manager employed by a pharmaceutical firm was paid £50 a week whereas the man who did the job previously had been paid £60. She brought industrial tribunal proceedings claiming that by virtue of section 1(1) and (2)(a) of the Equal Pay Act 1970, her contract of employment should be treated as if she were entitled to the same salary as her predecessor. The claim was upheld by the industrial tribunal and on appeal by the Employment Appeal Tribunal. The Court of Appeal on the interpretation of Article 119 asked for a preliminary ruling from the European Court of Justice.

HELD: (ECJ) Article 119 of the EEC Treaty applied directly to all forms of direct and overt discrimination as regards equal work and equal pay. The decisive test was whether there was a difference in treatment between a man and a woman performing equal work within the meaning of Article 119. The Article's scope was not limited to situations where men and women were doing the same work simultaneously. [1980] E.C.R. 1275

COMMENTARY

Lord Denning in a dissenting judgment in the original Court of Appeal hearing had argued that the Equal Pay Act should be given a purposive interpretation to give effect to the objects of Article 119 and thus a reference to the E.C.J. was not required. This approach is also that of the European Court of Justice which has now held in *Marleasing SA v. La Commercial Internacional de Alimentacion SA* (Case C-106/89) [1990] E.C.R. I-4135 that a purposive construction should be applied to national law whether the provisions in question were applied before or after the relevant Directive. See also *Webb v. EMO Cargo (U.K.) Ltd (No. 2)* [1995] 1 W.L.R. 1454

KEY PRINCIPLE: *European Communities Act 1972, s. 2(4)*

"The provision that may be made under subsection (2) above (which provides for implementation of Community obligations by secondary legislation) includes subject to Schedule 2 of this Act, any such provision (of any such extent) as might be made by Act of Parliament, and any enactment passed or to be passed, other than one contained in this part of this Act, shall be construed and have effect subject to the foregoing provisions of this section."

KEY PRINCIPLE: *This section is a principle of construction to be used wherever possible to construe U.K. legislation consistently with Community law.*

Garland v. British Rail Engineering Ltd

British Rail provided all employees with travel concessions while they were in its employment. They also gave concessions to former employees. Wives and dependent children of male former employees were also allowed concessions, but no concessions were made to partners of female former employees. A female employee complained that this arrangement discriminated against her. An industrial tribunal rejected her claim, but it was upheld on appeal by the Employment Appeal Tribunal. The tribunal decision was reversed by the Court of Appeal on the basis that British Rail was not contractually obliged to provide travel concessions. On her appeal to the House of Lords, the European Court was asked as a preliminary to determine whether the alleged discrimination infringed Article 119 of the EEC Treaty.

HELD: (HL) On its correct interpretation the national legislation gave entitlement to the benefits. [1983] 2 A.C. 751

COMMENTARY

The House of Lords had referred the matter to the European Court of Justice after the Court of Appeal had ruled that the woman was not the victim of unlawful discrimination under English law. The European Court of Justice ruled that her treatment was a violation of an enforceable Community right. When the case returned to the House of Lords it ruled that there was in fact no conflict between the relevant U.K. statute and Community law.

Lister v. Forth Dry Dock & Engineering Co. (in receivership)

Forth Dry Dock, a Leith ship-repair business, appointed a receiver. Two of its managers formed a new company, Forth Estuary which bought Forth Dry Dock from the receiver for £35,000. One and a half hours before the transfer, the receiver dismissed the 25 employees of Forth Dry Dock. After the transfer Forth Estuary took on new workers at lower pay. Twelve former employees succeeded in an industrial tribunal claim for unfair dismissal contrary to the Transfer of Undertakings (Protection of Employment) Regulations 1981. The Employment Appeal Tribunal affirmed the industrial tribunal decision, but it was reversed by the Court of Session. The employees appealed.

HELD: (HL), The regulations were enacted to comply with the Directive on transfer of undertakings so that the benefits and burdens of a contract of employment passed from the transferor to the transferee on the transfer of an undertaking. The Directive provided that the transfer of an undertaking should not constitute grounds for dismissing an employee. To construe the regulations on the basis that the employees had been dismissed before the transfer would mean that Parliament had failed to comply with the obligations imposed on it by the Directive. The court was entitled to apply a purposive construction to the Regulations in order to give effect to the United Kingdom's Treaty obligations and, where necessary, imply words appropriate to comply with those obligations. A transferee could not avoid his liability to employees of an undertaking by requesting the transferor to dismiss the employees before the transfer thus leaving the employees with a worthless remedy against an insolvent transferor. [1990] 1 A.C. 546

COMMENTARY
Lord Oliver referred to the fact that the "greater flexibility available to the court in applying a purposive construction to legislation designed to give effect to the United Kingdom's Treaty obligations enables the court 'where necessary' to supply by implication words appropriate to comply with those obligations." This went beyond the ordinary rules of construction applicable to a purely domestic stature and without reference to Treaty obligations.

KEY PRINCIPLE: *Purposive statutory construction should not be applied to legislation which was not introduced to comply with obligations under the EEC Treaty.*

Duke v. Reliance Systems Ltd
The applicant was obliged by her employer to retire in line with a policy that female employees retired at 60 and men at 65. She claimed discrimination under section 6(4) of the Sex Discrimination Act 1975. She also said that even if section 6(4) made it lawful to discriminate on grounds of sex in relation to retirement age, it should be construed so as to give effect to the Equal Treatment Directive.

HELD: (HL) The 1975 Act was not passed to give effect to the Equal Treatment Directive. It had been intended to preserve discrimination in retirement ages. Nothing in the European Communities Act 1972 required or allowed an English court to distort the meaning of a statute in order to conform with EEC law which was not directly applicable. [1988] A.C. 618

COMMENTARY
The applicant's employer was a private employer therefore she could not rely on the direct effect of the Equal Treatment Directive (see *Marshall v. Southampton and South West Hampshire Health Authority (No.1)* (Case 152/84) [1986] E.C.R. 723). The House of Lords could not accept that section 2(4) of the European Communities Act required it to distort the meaning of a British statute so as to achieve an equivalent

effect against a private employer. The House did not make a reference under Article 177 and its very narrow and much criticised interpretation should be contrasted with that of the European Court of Justice in *Marleasing SA v. La Commercial Internacional de Alimentacion SA* and its own judgment in *Webb v. EMO Air Cargo (U.K.) Ltd (No. 2)* (see page 19).

KEY PRINCIPLE: *The rule that an injunction cannot be granted against the Crown should be set aside if it prevents the granting of interim relief in a dispute governed by E.C. law.*

R. v. Secretary of State for Transport, ex p. Factortame (Case C-213/89)

A Spanish-owned company owned fishing vessels which were registered in the British merchant fleet. The Merchant Shipping Act 1988 established a new register open only to British-owned vessels. The Spanish-owned company failed to qualify for the register and challenged the provisions of the Act by way of judicial review. The Divisional Court referred to the European Court of Justice the question whether E.C. law affected the registration conditions which a Member State might impose on merchant shipping. The court granted the applicants an interim injunction disapplying the operation of the register and restraining the Secretary of State from enforcing the Act pending the European Court of Justice decision. The injunction was discharged on appeal by the Court of Appeal and the applicants appealed to the House of Lords, which held that under English law the courts had no jurisdiction to grant interim relief in terms that would involve either overturning a statute or granting an injunction against the Crown. The House referred to the European Court of Justice the issue whether Community law either obliged the national court to take interim steps to protect rights claimed or empowered the court to do so.

HELD: (ECJ) Where an application was made for interim relief in a case concerning Community law, a rule of national law must be set aside if the national court considered that rule to be the only obstacle to the grant of interim relief. [1990] E.C.R. I-2433

COMMENTARY
The House of Lords decided in the light of the European Court of Justice decision to uphold the injunction originally granted by the Divisional Court

The *Factortame* series of cases is of great importance in establishing that an Act of Parliament should not be implemented in part if it denies enforceable rights under Community law. To achieve this the rule that injunctions should not lie against the Crown was abrogated. The House of Lords in effect is acknowledging the primacy of E.C. law over national legislation. However, two qualifications should be born in mind. First, the whole statute was not repealed; only those sections which applied to E.U. nationals were not applied. Secondly, the case does not deal with a situation where Parliament was expressly and intentionally flouting a provision in E.C. law.

Secretary of State for Employment, ex p. Equal Opportunities Commission

The right not to be unfairly dismissed and to redundancy pay were limited by the Employment Protection (Consolidation) Act 1978 to employees working continuously for more than two years and more than eight hours a week. The Commission believed this to discriminate indirectly against women workers, more of whom worked part-time than men, and argued that this was a breach of the United Kingdom's obligations under the E.C. Treaty. The Commission asked the Secretary of State to do away with the discrimination and when he refused on the grounds that it was objectively justified sought judicial review of his refusal. The Divisional Court would not direct the Secretary of State to introduce legislation or declare that the United Kingdom was in breach of its treaty obligations. The statutory provisions were discriminatory but had been objectively justified. The Court of Appeal by a majority upheld the Divisional Court decision. The Commission appealed.

HELD: (HL) The Divisional Court had jurisdiction to declare that the 1978 Act was incompatible with E.C. law. The onus of showing that the discrimination was objectively justified was on the Secretary of State. That it brought about an increase in part-time work, as the Secretary of State claimed the measure had done, could be an objective justification of the statute. However, the evidence before the Divisional Court did not establish that the policy had resulted in any greater availability of part-time work. The 1978 provisions would be declared

incompatible with the E.C. Treaty and directives made under it
by the European Community. [1995] 1 A.C. 1

COMMENTARY
The House of Lords was here applying the principle derived
from *Factortame*.

---

3. THE EXECUTIVE (1)

Royal Prerogative

The prerogative is a discretionary power exercisable by the
government in certain spheres where Parliament has made
no provision.

KEY PRINCIPLE: *The courts may determine the extent of
prerogative powers.*

Burmah Oil v. Lord Advocate

During the Japanese invasion of Burma the army command
ordered that oil installations around Rangoon be destroyed so
they could not be used by the enemy. It was not disputed that
the destruction was lawful; it was assumed that it was carried
out in the exercise of the royal prerogative, and it was admitted
that the military situation at the time rendered the destruction
expedient for the defence of His Majesty's other territories. The
owners of the oil installations brought actions in Scotland
claiming to be entitled to compensation from public funds to
make good the damage sustained by them as result of the
destruction. On appeal from an order sustaining pleas against
relevancy, and dismissing the actions before trial, the Crown
cross-appealed that the actions were incompetent and should
be dismissed by virtue of the Public Authorities Protection Act
1893.

HELD: (HL) There was a legal right to some compensation
because if a subject was deprived of property through the
exercise of the royal prerogative for the benefit of the state,
he would generally be entitled to compensation at the public
expense. Battle damages was an exception to the general rule,
but the exception did not extend to destruction which was a

part of a deliberate long-term strategy (such as economic warfare) and would not have been done in any event for battle operations. The Public Authorities Protection Act 1893 did not invalidate the claim. [1965] A.C. 75

COMMENTARY
This case is an example of the use of the prerogative as an emergency power when inevitably in the face of unpredictable conditions its precise extent cannot always be stated in advance. Lord Reid said "the prerogative certainly covers doing all those things in an emergency which are necessary for the conduct of war." However, since the practice in modern years was to pass emergency statutory powers there were difficulties in applying the prerogative to modern conditions and "the prerogative is really a relic of a past age, not lost by disuse but only available for a case not covered by statute."

In the event the War Damage Act 1965 retrospectively provided that no person should be entitled to receive compensation for Acts of the Crown in destroying property during or in contemplation of war. Thus the judgment was effectively overruled by statute.

KEY PRINCIPLE: *Where power was conferred on the Crown by statute the Crown would have to take action under those powers not under equivalent pre-existing prerogative powers.*

Attorney-General v. de Keyser's Royal Hotel Ltd
During the First World War the Crown took possession of a hotel to be used as a Royal Flying Corps' headquarters. The owners gave up possession under protest and asked the court by a petition of right for a declaration that they were entitled to rent for the use and occupation of the premises, or to compensation.

HELD: (HL) The Crown was not entitled as of right, either under the prerogative or by statute, to take possession of a subject's land or buildings for administrative purposes in connection with the defence of the realm without paying compensation for their use and occupation. The hotel owner was not entitled to rent as there was no consensus on which to found a contract. [1920] A.C. 508

COMMENTARY

Lord Sumner in this case " . . . if there is adequate power to do all that is required under the statute, where is the emergency and public necessity which is the foundation for resort to the prerogative?" However, a somewhat different approach was taken in *R. v. Secretary of State for the Home Department, ex p. Northumbria Police Authority* (page 99) where the prerogative power to keep the peace supplemented powers available under the Police Act 1964.

Laker Airways Ltd v. Department of Trade

In 1972 the applicant company was granted a 10-year licence to operate an air service between London and New York. The start of the service was delayed by the need to obtain an American permit to run the service. This was done by designating the company as a carrier on that route and asking for a presidential permit. In February 1975 the state-owned airline applied unsuccessfully for the designation to be revoked. In July 1975 the Secretary of State for Trade announced a change of policy: only one U.K. airline would be allowed to operate on any long-haul route and accordingly the applicant's designation was withdrawn and the service would not be allowed to start. As a result the U.S. authorities withdrew their recommendation before the president had signed the permit. The applicant sought a declaration that the Department of Trade was not entitled to cancel the scheme. The judge granted the declaration and the Department appealed.

HELD: (CA) The Secretary of State was entitled to reverse the previous policy and could have done so by legislation. However, he had exceeded his authority by introducing the new policy as "guidance" since such guidance should be consistent with the general objectives laid down in the relevant statute. [1977] 1 Q.B. 643

COMMENTARY

Here the court for the first time went some way to acknowledging that the exercise as opposed to the extent of the prerogative might be reviewable. It held that even where a statute does not entirely cover a prerogative power that residual power must be exercised in a way that expresses the will of Parliament and the purpose of the statute (see also *R. v. Secretary of State for the Home Department, ex p. Fire*

Brigades Union, page 31). Lord Denning was prepared to see an even more robust role for the courts and argued that a prerogative should not be used "unreasonably or" mistakenly whether a statute covered it or not.

KEY PRINCIPLE: *Inferior courts and tribunals created under the royal prerogative are subject to judicial review*

R. v. Criminal Injuries Compensation Board, ex p. Lain

The widow of a police officer who had been shot dead on duty applied for compensation from the Board. The single board member who reviewed her case initially awarded her £300. She appealed, and three members of the board then decided that she was not entitled to any payment, because she had already received money from the police fund. She sought judicial review of the decision. The board claimed that it was effectively dispensing the bounty of the Crown and thus was not amenable to judicial review.

HELD: (DC) The board was a body of persons of a public, rather than a domestic, character. It had power to determine matters affecting subjects and a duty to act judicially. The fact that it was constituted under the prerogative and not by statute did not bar the court's jurisdiction. However, the board had not erred in offsetting the payments from the police fund against the applicant's entitlement. [1967] 2 Q.B. 864

COMMENTARY

The reasoning in this case was applied in the landmark GCHQ decision (*Council of Civil Service Unions v. Minister for the Civil Service*, page 29) which more clearly articulated the power of the courts to review the manner of the exercise as well as the existence of certain prerogative powers

---

KEY PRINCIPLE: *The treaty-making powers of the Crown are not reviewable.*

Ex p. Molyneaux

In 1985 the London and Dublin governments formed an Anglo-Irish conference concerned with Northern Ireland and its relations with the Republic Of Ireland. The applicants were

Unionists opposed to the agreement. They sought judicial review on the basis that it restricted the statutory powers and duties of the Secretary of State for Northern Ireland and would deprive subjects in Northern Ireland of some of the rights and privileges enjoyed by other U.K. citizens. They were refused leave to apply, but renewed their application before the single judge.

HELD: (QB) The Ireland Act 1949 expressly stated that the Republic was not to be regarded as a foreign power. The agreement did not deprive subjects in Northern Ireland of any privileges or place them on a different footing from other U.K. peoples. The Anglo-Irish conference would have no legislative or executive power and its establishment did not contravene any legal rule or statute or fetter the discretion of the Secretary of State. The conference had an international nature and the Anglo-Irish agreement concerned inter-state relations akin to a treaty, which were not justiciable. [1986] 1 W.L.R. 331

COMMENTARY

In *R. v. Secretary of State for Foreign and Commonwealth Affairs, ex p. Rees-Mogg* [1994] 2 W.L.R. 115 Lloyd L.J. dismissed the application for a declaration that by ratifying the Treaty on European Union the government transferred certain prerogative powers without statutory authority. However he accepted *obiter* that the principle of non-justiciability of certain aspects of the prerogative was not absolute and that section 6 of the European Parliament Election Act 1978 could require a court to consider whether any treaty the government proposed to ratify involved an increase in the powers of the European Parliament.

KEY PRINCIPLE: *The courts have power to determine whether a prerogative power exists. No new prerogative powers will be recognised.*

BBC v. Johns

The BBC appealed against a tax assessment, claiming Crown immunity from taxation. It claimed to be exercising, within the sphere of government, functions required or created for the purposes of government.

HELD: (CA) The Crown had never claimed broadcasting as part of the sphere of government. The BBC was independent and free from government control. The court would not create a new prerogative power. [1965] Ch. 32

COMMENTARY
Diplock L.J. "It is 350 years and a Civil War too late for the Queen's courts to broaden the prerogative." However since prerogative powers are so wide it is difficult for the courts to determine if and how ancient powers apply under new circumstances (see *R. v. Home Secretary, ex p. Northumbria Police Authority*, page 99)

KEY PRINCIPLE: *The courts may review the manner in which certain prerogatives are exercised.*

Council for Civil Service Unions v. Minister for the Civil Service (*GCHQ* case)
Mrs Thatcher as Minister for the Civil Service issued an order in council withdrawing from employees at the Government Communications Headquarters (GCHQ) the right to belong to a trade union. There had been no prior consultation with the unions or the employees. The Civil Service unions and six employees sought judicial review on the ground that the minister was under a duty to act fairly by consulting those affected. The single judge granted a declaration that the order was invalid. The Court of Appeal found for the Minister and the applicants appealed.

HELD: (HL) Merely because the Minister was exercising a prerogative power she was not immune from judicial review or freed from the duty to act fairly. Apart from considerations of national security, the applicants would have had a legitimate expectation of being consulted and the procedure adopted would have been unfair. However, it was for the executive to decide whether the requirements of national security outweighed fairness. The government had shown that the decision was based on considerations of national security which did outweigh fairness. [1985] 1 A.C. 374

COMMENTARY
The House attempted to set out guidelines for determining which powers of the prerogative were non-justiciable. In the

view of Lords Fraser and Brightman delegated powers emanating from prerogative power were not necessarily immune since the scope of such delegated powers would either expressly or impliedly be defined for example by reference to their object or the procedure by which they were to be exercised, with the result that such powers were subject to judicial control. In the view of Lords Scarman, Diplock and Roskill the controlling factor in determining whether the exercise of the power was the justiciability of its subject-matter rather than whether its source was the prerogative. Lord Roskill concluded that the following prerogatives would not be justiciable: the making of treaties, the defence of the realm, the grant of honours, the prerogative of mercy, the dissolution of Parliament and the appointment of ministers. Thus the justiciable prerogatives were essentially legal in character, involving either a legal right or legitimate expectation.

KEY PRINCIPLE: *The exercise of the prerogative of mercy is reviewable.*

R. v. Secretary of State for the Home Department, ex p. Bentley

The sister of a man hanged for murder in 1953 sought judicial review of the Home Secretary's decision to refuse him a posthumous pardon. In the course of argument it emerged that the substance of her case was that the Home Secretary had failed to recognise the fact that the prerogative of mercy was capable of being exercised in many different ways.

HELD: (DC) Such a failure to recognise the scope of the prerogative was reviewable. The court's powers could not be ousted simply by invoking the word "prerogative". The question was simply whether the nature and subject-matter of the decision was amenable to the judicial process. The prerogative was a flexible power which was now a safeguard against mistakes. The grant of a conditional pardon would be an acknowledgment by the State that a mistake had been made. The court would invite the Home Secretary to look again at the case. [1994] Q.B. 349

KEY PRINCIPLE: *The prerogative power of the issuing of passports is reviewable.*

R. v. Secretary of State for Foreign and Commonwealth Affairs, ex p. Everett

A British citizen living in Spain applied to the embassy for a new passport. He was told no passport would be issued, though the applicant could have a travel document to return to England. He was told that a warrant had been issued in England for his arrest and in these circumstances the government would not issue a new passport. It was only after he had begun judicial review proceedings against the Secretary of State that the applicant was given details of the warrant which had been issued. The judge held that the Secretary of State should have inquired whether there was any reason why the policy should not be applied in the applicant's case, and made an order of certiorari to quash the refusal of a passport. The Secretary of State appealed.

HELD: (CA) A decision whether or not to issue a passport was an administrative decision which affected the individual's rights and was unlikely to have foreign policy implications. It was thus reviewable, even though taken under the royal prerogative, so the court had jurisdiction. However, the Secretary of State was entitled to refuse to issue a passport where there was an outstanding warrant. The Secretary of State should have told the applicant the details of the warrant and informed him that he would consider any representation as to circumstances which might justify making an exception to the usual rule. [1989] 1 Q.B. 811

KEY PRINCIPLE: *The prerogative must not be exercised in a way which defeats the will of Parliament.*

R. v. Secretary of State for the Home Department, ex p. Fire Brigades Union

In 1964 the Crown under the prerogative introduced a Criminal Injuries Compensation Scheme. The Criminal Justice Act 1988 enacted the scheme, and provided that the Act would come into force on a day appointed by the Home Secretary. No appointment was made and the non-statutory scheme continued. In 1993 the Home Secretary announced the replacement of the existing scheme by a non-statutory tariff scheme. The union challenged the new scheme and sought declarations that the minister had acted unlawfully by failing to introduce the statutory scheme and that the tariff scheme was an abuse of his prerogative powers. The Court of Appeal refused the first direction but granted the second. The Secretary of State appealed and the union cross-appealed.

HELD: (HL) The Home Secretary was bound to consider whether to exercise his discretion under the 1988 Act to introduce the statutory scheme. The tariff scheme was inconsistent with the statutory scheme, and in introducing it the Home Secretary had acted unlawfully. But he had no legally enforceable duty to introduce the statutory scheme. [1995] 2 A.C. 513

COMMENTARY
The decision in this case underlines the continuing legislative role of Parliament. The prerogative should not be used to bring in a scheme other than one which conforms to the scheme originally envisaged. The argument of the dissenting minority was that Parliament could always change the scheme in future since the Minister had not put an end to it. This was not accepted since the Minister was contravening the will of Parliament at the time, albeit such contravention could later be reversed by statute.

KEY PRINCIPLE: *The court in reviewing a measure taken under the prerogative may question the Crown's claim that national security precludes entertaining the action.*

R. v. Secretary of State for the Home Department, ex p. Ruddock
A member of the Campaign for Nuclear Disarmament learned that his telephone had been tapped under a warrant from the Home Secretary. He sought judicial review of the Home Secretary's decision to sign the warrant on the basis that the phone had been tapped for party political purposes and the tapping had not followed published criteria. He claimed to have a legitimate expectation that the published criteria would be followed. The Secretary of State declined to confirm or deny the existence of any warrant. He contended the court should decline jurisdiction on grounds of national security and that the doctrine of legitimate expectation did not apply since the applicant was not supposed to know his phone was being tapped.

HELD: (QB) The duty of the court was to examine the evidence and consider whether the application was properly brought. Jurisdiction would not be declined just because the minister said national security was involved. The fact that the applicant was not supposed to know of the tapping made it more important that the minister should follow the criteria he had promised to apply. But there was no evidence that the information had been used for party political purposes and so the application failed. [1987] 1 W.L.R. 1482

COMMENTARY
Although the action failed it did confirm the principle established in GCHQ that the courts were entitled to scrutinise actions by the executive which failed to maintain legitimate expectations. The court went further than the decision in GCHQ in refusing to accept that its jurisdiction could be totally ousted because of dangers to national security.

4. THE EXECUTIVE (2)

Ministerial Responsibility

KEY PRINCIPLE: *It is for Parliament, in accordance with the convention of ministerial responsibility, and not the courts to require the Home Secretary to explain an administrative decision.*

Liversidge v. Anderson

The plaintiff was detained under regulation 18b of the Defence (General) Regulations 1939. The measure allowed administrative detention where the Secretary of State had reasonable cause to believe a person to have hostile associations. The plaintiff sought to compel the Secretary of State to reveal the reasons for his detention and took the matter on appeal to the House of Lords.

HELD: (HL) The court could not inquire whether in fact the Secretary of State had reasonable grounds for the necessary belief. The production by the Secretary of State of an order of detention, made by him and apparently regular and duly authenticated, was a defence to the action unless the plaintiff succeeded in showing the order itself to be invalid. [1942] A.C. 206

COMMENTARY
In this case the decision was influenced by the existence of the convention. Of course in many later cases discretionary powers of ministers have been challenged successfully in court and this case marks what is generally accepted as a low point of judicial activism in the face of administrative decision making.

Law Officers

KEY PRINCIPLE: *The Attorney-General alone has absolute discretion in deciding whether consent should be given to a relator action to restrain unlawful action by a public authority.*

Gouriet v. Union of Post Office Workers

The executive of the Union of Post Office Workers voted in January 1977 to call for a boycott of mail to South Africa as part of an international protest against apartheid. The plaintiff sought the Attorney-General's consent to act as plaintiff in relator proceedings for an injunction to restrain the union from taking the proposed action. The Attorney-General refused to authorise the plaintiff to do so, and the plaintiff issued a writ in his own name seeking an injunction, which was refused by the judge. On appeal he was granted an interim injunction and leave to join the Attorney-General as a defendant. He amended his pleadings at the resumed hearing to claim a permanent injunction against the union and declaration that the Attorney-General had wrongfully refused his assent. The Attorney-General sought to have the pleadings struck out on the grounds that his discretion to refuse his assent was absolute. The Court of Appeal by a majority held that it had no power to review the Attorney-General's decision, that the plaintiff was not entitled to a permanent injunction but could claim declarations. All parties appealed to the House of Lords.

HELD: (HL) Only the Attorney-General could sue on behalf of the public to prevent public wrongs: a private individual could not do so on behalf of the public. The courts had jurisdiction to declare public rights but only at the suit of the Attorney-General. There was no power to grant an interim injunction to the plaintiff, since he had no right to sue. [1978] A.C. 435

COMMENTARY
It is the task of the Attorney-General to protect the public interest and as such he has power to take action against public bodies to prevent actions threatening a class of citizens. This case settled conclusively that the Attorney-General does not have to justify his decisions whether or not to assert public rights in a civil action known as a relator action. Such an action is "at the relation" of an individual who lacks standing himself. The Attorney-General's decisions in this area may not be reviewed by the courts. The ruling in *Gouriet v. Attorney-General* covers all civil proceedings brought for a declaration or an injunction in respect of civil rights.

The Courts and Executive Bodies

KEY PRINCIPLE: *A non-governmental body which exercises public functions may be susceptible to judicial review.*

R. v. Panel on Takeovers and Mergers, ex p. Datafin 1987
(For facts see Chapter 6, page 65.)

HELD: (CA) Because of its public element, the panel was amenable to judicial review although it had no statutory or prerogative basis. But there were no grounds for review [1987] Q.B. 815

COMMENTARY
The great increase in the numbers of non-statutory bodies which carry out public functions has presented difficulties of legal accountability. Here the courts have shown a willingness to extend the scope of public law thus recognising that those with executive power over citizens' lives may be found outside the government, the civil service and local government.

KEY PRINCIPLE: *Central government and bodies which are emanations of state for the purpose of the direct applicability of Community Directives include bodies which provide a public service.*

Foster v. British Gas

Female workers for British Gas, a nationalised corporation, were required to retire at 60, though their male counterparts could continue to work to 65. They complained that this offended against the E.C. Equal Treatment Directive, even though the relevant section of the Sex Discrimination Act 1975 did not prohibit discrimination in retirement provision. The industrial tribunal ruled that the Directive could not be relied on directly by the applicants as the corporation was not a state body. The House of Lords referred to the European Court of Justice the question whether the corporation was a body against which the Directive was directly enforceable.

HELD: (ECJ) The Directive might be relied on in a claim for damages against a body, whatever its legal form, which provided a public service under the state and as a result had special powers beyond those of normal individuals. [1991] 1 Q.B. 405

COMMENTARY

The jurisprudence of the European Court of Justice has an increasing impact on the approach of the courts to executive actions. With the extent of privatised bodies and the proliferation of quangos it is significant that the European Court of Justice has adopted such a wide definition of a state body.

Local Authorities

KEY PRINCIPLE: *Local authorities owe a fiduciary duty to their ratepayers.*

Bromley London Borough Council v. Greater London Council

The Greater London Council voted to implement the "fares fair" policy, levying a supplementary rate to subsidise public transport by reducing fares. Bromley Council was refused judicial review of the Greater London Council decision, but the decision was reversed in the Court of Appeal. The Greater London Council appealed.

HELD: (HL) The Greater London Council owed a fiduciary duty to ratepayers to have regard to their interests and were under a statutory obligation to apply business principles to the conduct of public transport and had acted *ultra vires* the relevant legislation and in breach of its fiduciary duty. [1983] 1 A.C. 768

COMMENTARY
The case establishes that before embarking on significant spending a local authority must consider the rights of interested parties.

KEY PRINCIPLE: *A decision of a minister applying financial measures of a statute affecting local government finance would be subject to review only for bad faith, improper motive or manifest absurdity.*

R. v. Secretary of State for the Environment, ex p. Hammersmith & Fulham London Borough Council (see page 83)

COMMENTARY
The courts are understandably reluctant to adjudicate in the sensitive political area of central local government relations.

Public Interest Immunity

KEY PRINCIPLE: *The Crown's objection to the production of a document as evidence in legal proceedings will be allowed if it is against the public interest to produce it.*

Duncan v. Cammell Laird

The submarine Thetis sank during trials and relatives of the dead sued the builders. They sought discovery of documents relating to contracts between the builders and the Admiralty and salvage reports on the submarine. The government refused to allow discovery on the grounds that it would be against the public interest.

HELD: (HL) The minister's certificate that the matter was one of national security was conclusive and could not be questioned in the courts. Public interest immunity could be claimed on both the basis of the contents of the documents and of their forming part of a class of documents which should not be disclosed. [1942] A.C. 624

COMMENTARY

Public interest immunity was formerly known (as in this case) as "Crown Privilege". It has its origin in the Crown's original immunity from all proceedings by virtue of the royal prerogative. It followed from this that it could not be compelled to produce documents as evidence whether it was a party to the proceedings or not and whether the documents were in the Crown's possession or not. This case identified two types of claims: first, those based on the grounds that the contents of a particular document would injure the national interest for example by endangering national security or by prejudicing good diplomatic relations; and secondly, the claim that the document is one of a class of documents which must be withheld to ensure the proper functioning of the public service. The House of Lords' judgment has been criticised because of its contention that the minister's certificate was conclusive and furthermore because the second ground on which privilege could be claimed was too wide.

KEY PRINCIPLE: *The court will decide as a matter of substantive law whether a claim for non-disclosure should be upheld in the public interest.*

Conway v. Rimmer

A police officer was prosecuted for theft. The charge was dismissed. However, he was dismissed from the police force and brought an action for malicious prosecution against his former superintendent. He sought discovery of relevant documents from the Home Office, which claimed immunity on the basis of Crown privilege.

HELD: (HL) It was for the courts, not the Crown to decide whether or not evidence should be withheld from a court of law. The court had to weigh the public interest in not revealing the contents of sensitive documents against the public interest in a fair trial of the case. The court was entitled to inspect the documents in private to determine whether they should or should not be disclosed. [1968] A.C. 910

COMMENTARY

This landmark case indicates the transformation of the doctrine from Crown Privilege to public interest immunity since it emphasises that the court not the Crown has the final decision on disclosure. The court further indicated that the power to examine documents applied to contents and class claims. In *Rogers v. Home Secretary* the House of Lords indicated their objection to the use of the term Crown Privilege. There Lord Pearson said " . . . the expression Crown Privilege is not accurate, though sometimes convenient. The Crown has no privilege in the matter".

KEY PRINCIPLE: *The court's power to inspect documents for which immunity is claimed also covers high level state policy documents.*

Burmah Oil v. Bank of England

The bank rescued the oil company from financial difficulties on terms dictated by the government, including the transfer to the bank of the oil company's shares in British Petroleum. The oil company challenged the transfer arrangement in court, seeking a declaration that it was unconscionable and inequitable. It sought discovery of the relevant documents held by the bank. On government instructions the bank resisted discovery of 62 documents. The Attorney-General intervened in the case and the Chief Secretary to the Treasury certified that their production would be contrary to the public interest. Some of the documents related to the formulation of government policy, others to commercial and financial information communicated in confidence. By mistake six of the documents were sent by the bank's solicitors to the oil company's solicitors and were read by them. The judge upheld the Crown's claim for privilege without having read any of the documents but gave leave to appeal. The Court of Appeal read the documents before giving judgment and dismissed the appeal. The plaintiffs appealed to the House of Lords.

HELD: (HL) Without inspection of the documents, it was impossible to decide whether the balance of the public interest lay for or against disclosure. On inspection it was apparent that none of them contained matter of such evidential value as to make their disclosure necessary for the fair disposal of the case. They were relevant but their significance was not such as to override the objections to their being disclosed. [1980] A.C. 1090

COMMENTARY

The significance of this case is that unlike *Conway v. Rimmer* the documents involved were generated at high ministerial level. Furthermore, the House of Lords also showed its reluctance to acknowledge the legitimacy of class immunity. Finally, the argument that policy-making documents should be kept secret from the court because there was a need for candour in civil servants' advice given to ministers was largely dismissed. Lord Keith said: "The notion that any competent or conscientious public servant would be inhibited at all in the candour of his writings by consideration of the off chance that they might have to be produced in a litigation is in my opinion grotesque."

KEY PRINCIPLE: *There has to be a reasonable probability not just a speculation that documents would help the plaintiff or damage a defendant before the court will scrutinise a claim for immunity.*

Air Canada v. Secretary of State for Trade (No. 2)

The British Airports Authority at the direction of the Secretary of State imposed substantial rises in landing charges at Heathrow airport. The plaintiff airlines claimed the Secretary of State had acted *ultra vires* because the imposition of increases to reduce public sector borrowing was not a purpose authorised by the Airports Authority Act 1975. The Secretary of State refused discovery of communications between government ministers and ministerial briefs, having certified that it would be contrary to the public interest to produce them. The plaintiffs claimed the documents were essential for the fair disposal of the case and invited the court to inspect them to verify that this was so. The judge ordered the documents be produced for his inspection, and the Secretary of State appealed successfully to the Court of Appeal. The plaintiffs appealed to the House of Lords.

HELD: (HL) It was for the party seeking discovery to demonstrate that the information was likely to help his own case or damage that of his opponent. This applied both at the stage of private inspection by the judge and at the stage of ordering production to the other party. On the facts, the plaintiffs had not made out their case for the documents to be inspected. Cabinet minutes were entitled to a high degree of protection against disclosure but were not automatically immune from disclosure. [1983] 2 A.C. 394

COMMENTARY
Although this case does not deny the power of the courts to override claims by the executive to privilege, it does put more obstacles in the way of a litigant in his task of asking the court to order discovery. He cannot embark on a "fishing expedition".

KEY PRINCIPLE: *Discovery will be ordered when the rights of the litigant outweigh the possibility that a government ministry will face ill-judged or unfair comment.*

Williams v. Home Office
A prisoner was placed in a so-called control unit which involved 90 days of solitary confinement followed by 90 days of limited association with other prisoners. The Prison Rules allowed the Home Secretary to authorise the removal of a prisoner from association with other prisoners for one month and thereafter from month to month. The prisoner sued the Home Office for false imprisonment on the basis that by instituting a predetermined policy of 180 days' detention the Home Secretary had fettered his duty to review the situation before renewing the authority for his detention each month. The Home Office objected to certain documents being disclosed and claimed public interest immunity for 23 days which it claimed concerned the formulation of government policy. The Home Secretary claimed that the Home Office policy was irrelevant to the issue before the court and so discovery of the documents was unnecessary.

HELD: (QB) The Home Office could not claim public interest immunity on the ground that the candour of ministers and officials might otherwise be inhibited. The action extended to issues of fact, including whether the manner by which the monthly extensions were ordered was unreasonable. The liberty of the subject was at stake. The court inspected the documents and having done so ordered that six of them be produced. [1981] 1 All E.R. 1151

COMMENTARY

This case is a further undermining of the candour argument. There was however an implied undertaking that the documents would not be used for any other purpose than an action against the Home Office illustrating that public interest immunity is a matter of evidence concerned with discovery of documents for litigation not freedom of information generally.

KEY PRINCIPLE: *Sources that need to be protected include those involving authorised bodies as well as government departments.*

D v. National Society for the Prevention of Cruelty to Children

The NSPCC was informed that the respondent's baby daughter had been ill-treated and an inspector was sent to the family home. The information proved to be untrue, but the false accusation affected the respondent's health and she sought from the NSPCC the name of the informant with a view to suing the informant. She issued a writ against NSPCC claiming damages for failure to exercise reasonable care in its investigation and asked for discovery of her case file. The NSPCC resisted discovery but it was ordered by the Master. The judge reversed the Master's decision but it was reinstated by the Court of Appeal, on the grounds that only central government had the power to refuse discovery on the ground of public interest. The NSPCC appealed to the House of Lords.

HELD: (HL) The public interest required that persons who gave information about child abuse should remain anonymous, otherwise the information would dry up. The fact that the NSPCC was not under a legal duty to bring proceedings could not affect the degree of protection from discovery afforded to the NSPCC's informants. [1978] A.C. 171

COMMENTARY

Here by analogy with the law on police informants the public interest required confidentiality to those who gave information to the Society which was recognised under the Children and Young Persons Act. Confidentiality is not in itself a sufficient ground for non-disclosure but is a factor which the court can take into account in determining the balance of competing public interests.

See also *Alfred Crompton v. Customs and Excise (No.2)* [1974] A.C. 405.

Science Research Council v. Nassé

In the course of proceedings before an industrial tribunal for alleged discrimination, a complainant sought discovery of her own performance assessments and those of two colleagues she said had been selected for promotion in preference to her. The industrial tribunal ordered discovery in this and a similar case and in both cases the employer appealed. They argued that the disclosure of the performance assessments would breach confidence, damage industrial relations and impair the efficiency of promotion procedures.

HELD: (HL) It was a matter of discretion for the tribunal whether to order discovery of confidential reports or other documents relating to an employee. The tribunal should not order discovery unless it is necessary either for disposing fairly of the proceedings or for saving costs, and when exercising that discretion, in relation to confidential documents, it should have regard to the fact that the documents were confidential and the extent to which third party interests would be affected. The tribunal need not order discovery if the information could be obtained from other sources. If it was necessary for fairly disposing of the proceedings discovery must be ordered despite the confidential nature of the material. The tribunal should inspect the documents and consider whether they could be edited to exclude confidential but irrelevant parts. [1979] 3 All E.R. 673

KEY PRINCIPLE: *Documents arising from police complaints proceedings do not fit into a class covered by public interest immunity.*

R. v. Chief Constable of West Midlands Police, ex p. Wiley

The applicant was arrested and charged with robbery and shotgun offences. At his trial the prosecution offered no evidence and he complained against the police and brought an action against the chief constable. He declined to make a statement to the police under the complaints procedure without an undertaking that the information would not be used in

the civil action. The chief constable declined to give the undertaking and he obtained a declaration that the chief constable
had acted unlawfully in declining the undertaking. The chief
constable appealed.

The second applicant was arrested following a street fight
during which he had struck a plain clothes police officer. He
claimed he was seriously assaulted at the police station and
made a complaint. Both applicants refused to make any statements under the police complaints procedure without an
undertaking that the information would not be used in a civil
action. The chief constable declined to give the undertaking.
Popplewell J. held that the public interest immunity attached to
police complaints procedure as a class so as to prevent their
disclosure and the use of information therefrom in civil proceedings. He granted the declarations sought and in the second
case an injunction. The Court of Appeal dismissed the chief
constable's appeals.

HELD: (HL) The appeals were allowed. There was no clear
justification for imposing a general class public interest immunity on all documents by an investigation into a complaint
against the police. [1995] 1 A.C. 274.

COMMENTARY
Earlier authorities were overruled. The decision left open the
possibility of a contents claim based on the particular contents
of specific documents and furthermore that a class claim
might be upheld for a sub-class of documents (see Taylor v.
Anderton below). The decision was generally welcomed as
underlining that the case for a class claim must be clearly set
out and will not readily be accepted by the court.

KEY PRINCIPLE: *A class claim to non-disclosure may attach
to reports of police officers investigating complaints.*

Taylor v. Anderton
The plaintiff was acquitted of offences of dishonesty related to
business dealings. He began proceedings against the chief constable for malicious prosecution, misfeasance in public office
and conspiracy. During the proceedings he applied for production of reports prepared by investigating officers during inves-
tigations into police conduct which had taken place after his

acquittal. The chief constable asserted a class claim to public interest immunity.

HELD: (CA) Investigating officers should feel free to report on professional colleagues or members of the public without apprehension that their opinions might be disclosed. Public interest immunity attached to their reports. However, it was for the judge to determine whether their production was so essential to a fair disposition of the matter that the immunity should be overridden. [1995] 1 W.L.R. 447

KEY PRINCIPLE: *The balancing test of public interests also applies in claims for non-disclosure in criminal proceedings.*

R. v. Governor of Brixton Prison, ex p. Osman

The applicant was facing extradition to Hong Kong on charges of conspiracy, fraud and theft. Three applications for habeas corpus failed. In the course of the third application, correspondence between the magistrate's court and the Home Office and between the latter and the Hong Kong government was disclosed to the parties, though not read in open court. In his fourth application for habeas corpus the applicant relied on nine items in the correspondence and sought discovery of other documents. The Secretary of State claimed public interest immunity in the documents.

HELD: (DC) The proceedings were criminal in nature and public interest immunity could be claimed in criminal as well as civil proceedings. That immunity had to be balanced against the weighty interest of justice. None of the nine documents disclosed any matter which required that the privilege be set aside, and since there had only been limited dissemination of the documents they should not be disclosed. The applicant was also estopped from relying on the documents as they had been found irrelevant in the previous proceedings. [1991] 1 W.L.R. 281

COMMENTARY

There is a dearth of direct authority for claims of non-disclosure in criminal proceedings which is scarcely surprising since as Mann L.J. stated here "Where the interests of justice arise in a criminal case touching and concerning liberty, or conceivably on occasion life, the weight to be attached to the interests of justice is plainly very great indeed". The collapse of the Matrix Churchill trial followed the refusal of the trial judge to accept ministers' public interest immunity certificates in a criminal prosecution. In *R. v. Ward* [1993] 1 W.L.R. 619 the Court of Appeal confirmed that the prosecution in a criminal case has a duty generally to disclose all the evidence which it has gathered but this was subsequently overridden by statute.

5. PARLIAMENT

KEY PRINCIPLE: *The election of M.P.s is governed by statute.*

R. v. Boundary Commission for England, ex p. Foot

The Boundary Commission were on the point of delivering a report under the House of Commons (Redistribution of Seats) Acts 1949–1979. Leading members of the Labour Party, and three local authorities, sought judicial review of the Commission's proposals for revised parliamentary boundaries. The grounds of review in the first application were that the Commission had failed to give effect to the principle of equal representation for electors embodied in the requirement that "the electorate of any constituency shall be as near the electoral quota as possible" contained in one of the rules scheduled to the 1949 Act. In the local authorities' application it was claimed that the Commission had wrongly decided that they were bound to recommend 13 constituencies in Tyne and Wear. The Divisional Court dismissed both applications and the applicants appealed.

HELD: (CA) Dismissing the first appeal, that the High Court had power to review the carrying out by the Commission of instructions given to them by Parliament. The 1949 rules had been reduced by an Act of 1958 to the status of guidelines. The work of the Commission necessarily involved subjective views so that there was a heavy burden on anyone seeking judicial review of their decisions. The court might have made a declaration, but relief by way of an order of prohibition was not appropriate. In the second case, the assistant commissioner had in his report recorded the proposal from the local authorities that there should be 14 constituencies. He had recommended against the proposal and his report had been accepted by the Commission so there was no ground for judicial review. [1983] 1 Q.B. 600

COMMENTARY
The Boundary Commission was set up by Act of Parliament with power to make recommendations for changes in boundaries of parliamentary constituencies. The requirement of proportionality in respect of size was a guideline which could not be enforced against the Commissioners. The fact that their recommendations might benefit one political party more than another was not sufficient grounds to review the recommendations.

KEY PRINCIPLE: *The franchise is not dependent on property. Residence for the purposes of the electoral laws means factually resident at the appropriate time.*

Fox v. Stirk and Bristol Electoral Registration Officer; Ricketts v. Cambridge City Electoral Registration Officer

Two students, one at Bristol and the other at Cambridge University, appealed to the local county courts against a decision of the registration officer that since they were not "resident" in the respective constituencies on October 10, 1969 they could not be included on the electoral register there. Both students had arrived for the start of term before October 10 and were living in university accommodation. In both cases the county court upheld the officers' decisions.

HELD: (CA) The students were not only factually resident in the particular constituency on the qualifying date, they were also resident for the purposes of the Representation of the People Act 1949 because they had a sufficient degree of permanence in their residence. A person might be resident in more than one place and could register in those places to vote although he could only vote once at a general election. [1970] 2 Q.B. 463

Hipperson v. Newbury District Electoral Registration Officer

Seven women who were camped outside a military airfield in protest against nuclear weapons were included in the electoral register for the local constituency. At the time the women, who had lived in the camp for up to two years, were facing eviction proceedings brought by the Department of Transport and the local authority. An objection was lodged to their registration and upheld by the registration officer on the basis that the unlawfulness of their residence disqualified them from inclusion on the register. The county court upheld an appeal by the women and the objector appealed.

HELD: (CA) The franchise was not based on considerations of the standard of accommodation of the would-be voter. All the women had been on the site for a considerable period and it was immaterial that they might be required to leave shortly after registration. The issue as to whether a person was resident in a particular place was a question of fact to be determined by the tribunal of fact. There were no grounds for the court to interfere. The appeal would be rejected. [1985] Q.B. 1060

KEY PRINCIPLE: *Limits on spending under electoral law apply to individual constituencies. Organisations and parties can spend freely on national campaigns without infringing the law.*

R. v. Tronoh Mines Ltd

During the 1951 general election campaign, a company placed advertisements which condemned Labour party policy, with particular reference to controls on company dividends. The advertisement said Labour should be rejected in favour of "a new and strong government with ministers who may be relied upon to encourage business enterprise and initiative". The company was charged with unlawfully incurring expenses with a view to promoting the election of a parliamentary candidate in the constituency where the company had its offices and the newspaper was published.

HELD: (CCC) Section 63 of the Representation of the People Act 1949 under which the company was charged, was designed to outlaw spending on adjustments supporting a particular candidate in a particular constituency. The advertisement was aimed at supporting the interests of a party in all constituencies and there was no case to answer. [1952] 1 All E.R. 697

COMMENTARY

The decision illustrates the different approaches to spending at constituency and national level. For a recent case on a similar point see *Walker v. Unison* [1995] S.L.T. 1226. It is argued that this favours the wealthier political parties.

KEY PRINCIPLE: *Members of Parliament (including members of the House of Lords) enjoy immunity from arrest for civil process.*

Stourton v. Stourton

The wife of a peer of the realm brought proceedings against her husband, from whom she was separated, for the return of property belonging to her under the Married Women's Property Act 1882. The husband was ordered to return certain items of property and to complete a questionnaire from the wife. He failed to do so and she issued a writ of attachment. The peer claimed privilege against attachment.

HELD: (Probate Division) Whether or not parliamentary privilege arose and if it did what was its scope and effect, were issues to be determined by the court in accordance with the common law, not with parliamentary practice. The privilege from arrest of a Member of Parliament related only to civil process, that is to say, arrest to compel performance of a civil obligation. The wife was seeking to compel the husband to perform such an obligation, so he was protected by parliamentary privilege. [1963] P. 302

KEY PRINCIPLE: *The courts will not review the internal proceedings of Parliament itself.*

Bradlaugh v. Gossett

The plaintiff, Charles Bradlaugh, was elected M.P. for Northampton. On previous occasions he had refused to take the oath in the prescribed form. When he required the Speaker to call him to the table to take the oath, the Sergeant-at-Arms, in pursuit of a resolution of the House, prevented him from doing so. The plaintiff sought an injunction against the Sergeant-at-Arms.

HELD: (QBD) The House of Commons was not subject to the control of the courts in relation to matters concerning its internal procedures. Thus, a court could not inquire into whether it was proper for the House to restrain a member from doing within the walls of the Commons something which by the general law he was entitled to do, namely to take the oath prescribed by the Parliamentary Oaths Act 1866. No action lay against the Sergeant-at-Arms for excluding a member in accordance with a resolution of the House. (1884) 12 Q.B.D. 271

COMMENTARY

The Bill of Rights 1689 provides that "the freedom of speech and debates or proceedings in Parliament ought not to be impeached or questioned in any court of law or place out of Parliament". This provision was invoked by the judge to halt a libel case brought by Neil Hamilton M.P. against *The Guardian* newspaper which had accused him of accepting cash for asking questions in the Commons. A new clause in the Defamation Act 1996 tabled by Lord Hoffman in the House of Lords amended the Bill of Rights to allow an M.P. to waive privilege. Hamilton was able to reopen the case but was soon forced to withdraw from the action.

KEY PRINCIPLE: *The courts have the power to determine the limits of the privileges of the House of Commons but the Commons have exclusive jurisdiction within those limits.*

Stockdale v. Hansard

Inspectors of Prisons reported to the House of Commons that at Newgate prison they had found "a book of a most disgusting nature" with "plates . . . indecent and obscene in the extreme". The reference was to a textbook on the female reproductive system written by a medical practitioner whose publisher sued for libel. The inspectors claimed that the book was never considered a scientific work but was "intended to take young men in by inducing them to give an exorbitant price for an indecent work". The inspectors pleaded parliamentary privilege, relying on a resolution of the House of Commons.

HELD: (QB) It was no defence that the libel was part of a document which was, by order of the House of Commons, laid before the House and the court would determine whether the House had the privileges claimed. (1839) 9 Ad. & E. 1

COMMENTARY
Parliament later passed an Act giving immunity from action for defamation to papers or reports certified to have been printed by the authority of of either House or Parliament. As a result the action was stayed, the court refusing to look behind the Speaker's certificate that the inspectors' report was subject to the Act.

KEY PRINCIPLE: *The Conservative Party is not an unincorporated association.*

Conservative Central Office v. Burrell (Inspector of Taxes)

The Conservative Party was assessed for corporation tax on its income from funds between 1972 and 1976. The party appealed on the basis that it was not an unincorporated association and so not a company within the meaning of the relevant Act. Revenue commissioners found it was an unincorporated association but their decision was overturned by Vinelott J. The Crown appealed.

HELD: (CA) An unincorporated association was an association between two or more persons bound together for one or more common purposes by mutual undertakings, each having mutual duties and rights. Its rules identified where its control rested and the terms on which people could become or cease to be members. There had to be a contract and on the facts there was no such contract between the members of the local constituency association and M.P.s, so that the party lacked the characteristics of an unincorporated association for the purposes of the taxing statutes. The appeal would be dismissed. [1982] 1 W.L.R. 522

COMMENTARY
The status of political parties is little dealt with by law. They are not even recognised by Hansard, the Official Report of the House, which refers to M.P.s by name and constituency.

Delegated Legislation

KEY PRINCIPLE: *Fairness is not applicable in the legislative process.*

Bates v. Lord Hailsham of St Marylebone

A committee acting under the Solicitors Act 1957 produced a draft order dealing with solicitors' fees. A solicitors's association brought an action for an injunction because it had not been consulted about the fees changes.

HELD: Considerations of natural justice did not apply to the legislative function. The Lord Chancellor was under no duty to consult those who would be affected. [1972] 1 W.L.R. 1373

COMMENTARY
Megarry J. held that the function of making the order was legislative rather than executive or administrative. He said "I do not know of any implied right to be consulted or make objections, or any principle on which the courts may enjoin the legislative process at the suit of those who contend that insufficient time for consultation and consideration has been given". This was a controversial decision and some commentators have argued that the making of the order was an administrative rather than a legislative act and that it could be said to be in accordance with good administration for the court to impose a duty to consult in making general rules.

KEY PRINCIPLE: *A statutory instrument is complete from the moment that it is made and laid before Parliament.*

R. v. Sheer Metalcraft
Sheer Metalcraft Ltd were charged with selling excess goods in contravention of a statutory instrument. They pleaded that the instrument was invalid because the provisions of the Statutory Instruments Act 1946 and regulations made under it for the printing of statutory instruments had not been complied with.

HELD: (Streatfield J.) The statutory instrument was valid and effective as soon as made or where it is required to be laid before Parliament as soon as that is done, regardless of whether the Act has been complied with. [1954] 1 Q.B. 586

COMMENTARY
The question of whether publication of delegated legislation is necessary for it to be valid has been a subject of much debate. On the facts here since the instrument had been brought to the attention of the defendant by means other

than publication the court did not have to decide on whether publication was necessary. A further complication is that the duty to publish may be directory or mandatory depending on the parent legislation.

6. JUDICIAL REVIEW—PROCEDURE

Time Limits

KEY PRINCIPLE: *An application for judicial review shall be made promptly and in any event within three months from the date when grounds for the application first arose unless the court considers that there is a good reason for exceeding the period within which the application shall be made. Rules of the Supreme Court, Ord. 53, r. 4.*
Supreme Court Act 1981, s. 31 (6):

"Where the High Court considers that there has been undue delay in making an application for judicial review, the court may refuse to grant: (a) leave for the making of the application; or (b) any relief sought on the application, if it considers that the granting of the relief sought would be likely to cause substantial hardship to, or substantially prejudice the rights of, any person or would be detrimental to good administration."

KEY PRINCIPLE: *The time limit referred to the leave stage; although an application had to be made promptly the court had discretion to grant leave. Undue delay could include situations within the three months.*

R. v. Stratford-on-Avon District Council, ex p. Jackson 1985

Application for leave to seek judicial review was delayed for nine months. The delay was caused by securing legal aid and was not the applicant's fault.

HELD: (DC) Time should be extended but the court would still have discretion to consider the delay at the substantive hearing. [1985] 1 W.L.R. 1319

R. v. Secretary of State for Health, ex p. Furneaux

Doctors were granted outline consent to run a pharmacy but an appeal by local pharmacists was allowed. Six months later, the doctors sought judicial review on the grounds that the Minister had considered information of which they were unaware. The review was quashed on the intervention of a local company which had bought the only nearby pharmacy on the strength of the Minister's decision.

HELD: If an applicant for judicial review failed to apply promptly he was guilty of undue delay even if there was a reason. The court then had a discretion to refuse judicial review on the ground of substantial prejudice to the rights of another, which need to have a causal connection with the delay [1994] 2 All E.R. 652.

COMMENTARY
Courts have stressed the need for speed in judicial review of public authorities. They should not be kept in suspense about the legal validity of their decisions, and there are practical considerations, including the effect of uncertainty on budget decisions. The rules lay down a three-month time limit for applications. In certain circumstances applications made within three months can be dismissed for delay. There is a discretion to extend the time limit. The courts are reluctant to dismiss an application on grounds of delay where a private citizen is defending himself against an unfounded claim by a public body (*Wandsworth London Borough Council v. Winder*, see page 60).

Sufficient Interest

KEY PRINCIPLE: *Supreme Court Act 1981, s. 31(3):*

> "No application for judicial review shall be made unless the leave of the High Court has been obtained in accordance with rules of court; and the court shall not grant leave to make such an application unless it considers that the applicant has a sufficient interest in the matter to which the application relates."

KEY PRINCIPLE: *Except in cases where the applicant clearly lacked a sufficient interest the court should not treat* *the issues on standing as a preliminary one to be dealt with only at the leave stage but should consider it along with the merits of the case.*

R. v. Inland Revenue Commissioners, ex p. National Federation of Self-Employed and Small Businesses Ltd

The Federation sought a declaration that the Inland Revenue had acted unlawfully in making an arrangement with Fleet Street casual printworkers that it would not investigate arrears of unpaid tax provided the casuals registered in future. It maintained this was different from the way the revenue treated other self-employed and small business people.

HELD: (HL) It was necessary in determining whether an applicant had sufficient interest to identify the matter to which the application related. Sufficient interest, except in cases where there was obviously none, should be treated as a possible reason for refusal of discretionary relief, rather than as a preliminary issue or a matter of jurisdiction. [1982] A.C. 617.

COMMENTARY
This case marked a liberalisation of the approach of the courts to leave although it clearly demonstrated that even if the applicant is granted leave he can still be shown at the substantive hearing to have no standing. The court stressed that the law should not allow a reversion to technical restrictions on locus standi which had been current thirty years before.

KEY PRINCIPLE: *Where individuals did not have sufficient interest they could not obtain it by forming themselves into an association.*

R. v. Secretary of State for the Environment, ex p. Rose Theatre Trust

Developers of a site in central London discovered the remains of an Elizabethan theatre. A trust company was set up with a view to preserving the remains for public exhibition. The Secretary of State declined to list the remains as a building of historic importance. The trust sought judicial review.

HELD: (QB) The Secretary of State's decision was a government decision in respect of which members of the public had insufficient interest to bring review proceedings. A member of the public did not obtain a sufficient interest by applying to the Secretary of State and receiving a reply. The members of the trust had no standing as individuals and had created none by getting together. [1990] 1 Q.B. 504

COMMENTARY
The court here refused to acknowledge that a number of persons who oppose a administrative decision but who individually lack standing can create sufficient interest by becoming a pressure group.

KEY PRINCIPLE: *Pressure groups may have standing, each case being decided on its own merits.*

R. v. H.M. Inspectorate of Pollution, ex p. Greenpeace (No. 2)
The applicant sought judicial review of the inspectorate's decision to vary the licence of the Sellafield nuclear plant to expand reprocessing of nuclear waste.

HELD: (QB) The applicant was a respected body with a genuine interest in the issues raised. It had 2,500 supporters in the area where the plant was situated, who might not otherwise have an effective access to the court. The applicant had been actively involved in the consultation process relating to expansion of the plant. Accordingly, the applicant had a "sufficient interest in the matter" to be allowed to seek judicial review. [1994] 4 All E.R. 329

R. v. Secretary of State for Foreign and Commonwealth Affairs, ex p. World Development Movement Ltd
The applicants sought judicial review of the Secretary of State's decision to grant funding under section 1(1) of the Overseas Development and Co-operation Act 1980 for a project to construct a power station on the Pergau river, Malaysia. The decision had been taken against the advice of the Overseas Development Administration which had concluded it was an abuse of the statutory aid programme. The Secretary of State argued among other things that the World Development Movement did not have a sufficient interest to bring the application.

HELD: (DC) Since standing went to jurisdiction it should not be treated as a preliminary issue but was to be taken in the legal and factual context of the whole case. The merits of the challenge were important and the court should take account of the importance of vindicating the rule of law, the likely absence of other challengers and the nature of the breach which was complained of. On the evidence the project had no developmental promotion purpose within section 1(1) of the 1980 Act and the Secretary of State's decision was unlawful. [1995] 1 W.L.R. 386

COMMENTARY
Here the Court accepted that a political pressure group may have sufficient standing dependent on the circumstances. This case applied the dicta in *The National Federation of Self-Employed Case* (see page 55). It stressed also that the applicants were an established organisation with a prominent role and experience in the matters under review.

KEY PRINCIPLE: *An individual and a group set up by statute may both have standing.*

R. v. Secretary of State for Employment, ex p. Equal Opportunities Commission

The Equal Opportunities Commission wrote to the Secretary of State pointing out that the exclusion of certain part-time employees from the protection against unfair dismissal provided by the Employment Protection (Consolidation) Act 1978 discriminated against women because considerably more women than men worked part-time. The EOC claimed they infringed the EEC Treaty and Directives. The Secretary of State claimed the legislation was justifiable. On the EOC's application for judicial review the Divisional Court held that both the EOC and a part-time worker who had failed to meet the Act's qualifying conditions had standing, but refused to order the Secretary of State to introduce legislation or to declare that the United Kingdom was in breach of relevant obligations under the EEC Treaty. Both applicants appealed.

Held: (HL) The part-time worker's claim for redundancy pay ought to have been brought against her employer before an industrial tribunal and not in the Divisional Court. The EOC had a sufficient interest in the proceedings to give it standing, since its duty under the Sex Discrimination Act 1975 was to work towards the elimination of discrimination. The Secretary of State had failed to show that the exclusion of part-time workers had resulted in a greater availability of part-time work, so had failed to justify the exclusion. It would be declared incompatible with the EEC Treaty and Directives. [1995] 1 A.C. 1

COMMENTARY
This case illustrates the stand the court will take in cases where both an individual and a group have an interest in a given decision. In cases where a group is set up by statute to uphold a certain interest the court may prefer the group.

Public or Private Law

KEY PRINCIPLE: *As a general rule public law rights must be enforced by way of judicial review in the procedure provided for in Order 53 against public authorities, rather than by way of writ or originating summons.*

O'Reilly v. Mackman
Four prisoners were disciplined by the prison board of visitors for offences arising out of a riot. Three brought action against the visitors by writ in the Queen's Bench Division and one by summons in the Chancery Division seeking declaration and injunction. The defendants' applications to strike out the actions were dismissed at first instance but allowed by the Court of Appeal. The plaintiffs appealed to the House of Lords.

HELD: (HL) The reform of Rules of the Supreme Court Order 53 had removed unfair disadvantages to applicants for judicial review which had in the past made applications for prerogative orders an inadequate remedy. Order 53 protected decision-making public bodies against groundless, unmeritorious or tardy harassment. It would be contrary to public policy and an abuse of the process of the court for a person seeking to establish that a decision of a public authority infringed his public law to proceed by way of ordinary action and thus evade those protections. Exceptions should be decided on a case-by-case basis. [1983] 2 A.C. 237

COMMENTARY
The House was concerned to provide safeguards against frivolous applications in public law matters and considered

therefore that Order 53 procedure would generally be the most appropriate method. One consideration was that there was a need for a consistent treatment of such cases and this was already being developed in the Divisional Court. The House did however accept that there might be occasions where Order 53 procedure might not be appropriate. Such situations included cases where the public law matter was collateral to another application, cases where it was raised as a defence and finally the issue should be looked at on a case-by-case basis. Subsequent cases showed that there are exceptions to this general rule of exclusivity.

KEY PRINCIPLE: *Where a public body has public law deci-sion-making functions the determination of which was a necessary precedent to a private law right the public law decision can only be challenged by proceedings brought under Order 53. Private law actions should be brought by writ.*

Cocks v. Thanet District Council

A homeless person who had been given temporary accommo-dation by this local authority started proceedings against the authority in the county court claiming that they were in breach of their duty to house him permanently under the Housing (Homeless Persons) Act 1977. A High Court judge decided that the plaintiff was entitled to proceed with the claim in the county court rather than proceed by way of application for judicial review under R.S.C., Ord. 53. The council appealed directly to the House of Lords.

HELD: (HL) Where a person claimed that a public authority had infringed his public law rights it was as a general rule contrary to public policy and an abuse of process to allow him to proceed by way of ordinary action. That rule applied where a plaintiff was obliged to impugn a public authority's determina-tion as a condition precedent to enforcing a statutory private law right. In this case the private law matter of the statutory duty to house a homeless person arose only after the authority had determined that the person was homeless. This was a public law matter and the general rule should apply. [1983] 2 A.C. 286

Davy v. Spelthorne Borough Council

The council served the plaintiff with an enforcement notice under the Town and Country Planning Act 1971. He did not appeal against the notice within the statutory time-limit and so was unable to challenge it. However, he claimed that the reason he had not appealed was the council's negligent advice and he brought proceedings by writ for damages for negligence and for an injunction ordering the council not to implement the notice and an order setting it aside. The defendants' application to have the writ struck out was dismissed at first instance, but the Court of Appeal struck out the claims for injunction and setting aside of the enforcement notice on the ground that they raised public law questions and should be brought by way of judicial review under R.S.C., Ord. 53. The defendants sought to have the rest of the claim struck out on the same grounds.

HELD: (HL) The plaintiff's action for damages for negligence did not raise any issue of public law since he was not seeking to impugn a determination by a public body but bringing an ordinary action in tort in respect of which the procedure of R.S.C., Ord. 53 would be entirely inappropriate. There was no abuse of process in bringing that part of the claim by way of ordinary action rather than under R.S.C., Ord. 53. The order of the Court of Appeal would stand. [1984] 1 A.C. 262.

COMMENTARY
These two cases show differing conclusions being drawn by the House of Lords. These resulted from the application of the test in *O'Reilly v. Mackman*: could and should the action be brought by an application for judicial review? In *Cocks* the answer was yes, in *Davy*, no.

KEY PRINCIPLE: *A public law matter could be raised as a defence in a private claim without going through Order 53 procedure.*

Wandsworth London Borough Council v. Winder

The tenant of a council flat, while continuing to pay his original rent, refused to pay rent increases which he considered excessive. The council brought proceedings in the county court to recover the arrears and for possession of the flat. The tenant claimed in his defence that he was not liable to pay the arrears because the council's resolutions raising the rent were *ultra vires* and void and counter-claimed for a declaration to that effect. The council applied to strike out the defence and counter-claim as an abuse of process. The judge held it to be an abuse of process and contrary to public policy to challenge the conduct of a public authority other than by way of R.S.C., Ord. 53 procedure. The Court of Appeal by a majority allowed the appeal. The council appealed.

HELD: (HL) The private citizen's recourse to the courts for the determination of his rights was not to be excluded except by clear words. Nothing in the language of R.S.C., Ord. 53 or the Supreme Court Act 1981 could be taken as abolishing a citizen's right to challenge the decision of a local authority in the course of defending an action. [1985] A.C. 461.

COMMENTARY
The court observed that it would be a strange use of language to call the defendant's behaviour an abuse of the court process. He had not selected the procedure to be adopted and was merely seeking to defend the proceedings brought against him on the ground that he was not liable for the whole sum claimed. He put forward his defence as a matter of right, whereas in an application for judicial review success would require an exercise of the court's discretion in his favour.

KEY PRINCIPLE: *Private law rights can be enforced by private law action even if they involve a challenge to a public body's decision.*

Roy v. Kensington and Chelsea and Westminster Family Practitioner Committee
The Family Practitioner committee withheld fees from a general practitioner on the basis that he had failed to devote a substantial amount of time to general practice as required under the relevant National Health Service regulations. The general practitioner brought an action in the Queen's Bench Division to recover the fees. On the committee's application the judge struck out the action as an abuse of process, as the committee's decision was a matter of public law which could only be challenged by way of judicial review under R.S.C., Ord. 53. The Court of Appeal, however, held that the general practitioner had a contract for services with the committee so that his proper remedy was by way of ordinary action. The committee appealed.

HELD: (HL) A litigant possessed of a private law right could seek to enforce that right by ordinary action whether or not the proceedings would involve a challenge to a public law act or decision. The general practitioner's relationship to the committee conferred on him private law rights to fees and the bringing of an ordinary action to enforce that right did not constitute an abuse of process. [1992] 1 A.C. 624

COMMENTARY

The plaintiff would not be excluded from bringing the action even if there was no contract between him and the committee. He could sue if he had any sort of private law right. Lord Lowry referred to two different applications of the principle in *O'Reilly v. Mackman*: first, a broad approach under which Order 53 would be required if private rights were not in issue and secondly a narrow approach which required all applicants to proceed by Order 53 in all proceedings in which public law matters are raised, apart from the exceptions already noted. Lord Lowry, favouring the broad approach said, "unless the procedure adopted by the moving party is ill suited to dispose of the question at issue, there is much to be said in favour of the proposition that a court having jurisdiction ought to let a case be heard rather than entertain a debate concerning the form of the proceedings." This case is significant both in recognising that a single claim could be a mixture of public and private law and for moving away from a rigid approach to procedure.

KEY PRINCIPLE: *Disputes over dismissal involving public authorities are rarely suitable for judicial review.*

R. v. East Berkshire Health Authority, ex p. Walsh

A senior nursing officer was dismissed for misconduct by a district nursing officer and sought judicial review. The grounds of review were that the district nursing officer had no power to dismiss him and that he had been denied natural justice. The judge ruled on a preliminary point raised by the health authority that judicial review was appropriate because of the public interest in seeing that a public service acted lawfully towards its employees. The judge also ruled that it would be appropriate to allow the proceedings to continue under R.S.C., Ord. 53 as if they had been begun by writ. The health authority appealed.

HELD: (CA) An applicant for judicial review had to show that a public law right which he enjoyed had been infringed. The employee of a public body whose terms were controlled by statute might have rights in public as well as private law, but an infringement of statutory provisions giving rise to public law rights had to be distinguished from a breach of the contract of employment. The applicant was seeking to enforce a private law right under his employment contract and his application was a misuse of the judicial review procedure. The only remedy he was seeking was certiorari which was not available in a civil action so the proceedings could not be allowed to continue as if they had been begun by writ. [1985] 1 Q.B. 152

COMMENTARY
The mere presence of a public interest does not make the matter concerned a matter of public law. Most disputes about dismissal are private law disputes between the employer and the employee, even where the employer is a public body. They mostly belong in the industrial tribunal, not the Divisional Court.

KEY PRINCIPLE: *Where the applicant does not have a contract of employment judicial review may be an appropriate way to challenge a dismissal.*

R. v. Secretary of State for the Home Department, ex p. Benwell
The Dartmoor branch of the Prison Officers' Association passed a motion of no confidence in the prison governor. The motion was reported in the press. The branch chairman was warned that if spoke to the press about the governor he would be disciplined. He was ordered to attend a meeting with the regional director of the Prison Service but because of a dispute over the expenses of the journey did not attend. A disciplinary inquiry recommended a severe reprimand, but the Home Department gave him notice of dismissal. He appealed first to a single adjudicating officer and then to the Civil Service Appeal Board. At both appeals details of his disciplinary record, including the warning over press interviews, were before the tribunal, though they should have

been excluded under the terms of the disciplinary code and the applicant was not given a chance to put his claim that he had merely told the press the result of the branch meeting. He sought judicial review.

HELD: As a prison officer the applicant held the office of constable and had no private law rights that could be enforced in civil proceedings. The court had jurisdiction over the application of the code of conduct which was made under statute and prison rules. The applicant had been denied natural justice and the dismissal would be quashed. [1985] 1 Q.B. 554

COMMENTARY
These cases illustrate that a number of difficulties remain in deciding when Order 53 procedure is appropriate. There is a fear of opening the floodgates if public employees are allowed to pursue employment law matters by judicial review. However, the problem of deciding which cases are appropriate is seen for example in *Council of Civil Service Unions v. Minister for the Civil Service* (see p. 29) which on one interpretation could be said to be an employment law matter.

KEY PRINCIPLE: *A choice of procedure may be based partly on whether it would be suitable for the type of claim.*

Mercury Communications Ltd v. Director General of Telecommunications
In a dispute over the terms of their licence to run a telecommunications system, the plaintiffs issued an originating summons against the Director General seeking a declaration of the true terms of the licence. The judge dismissed the Director General's summons to have the action struck out as an abuse of process. The Court of Appeal allowed the Director General's appeal. The plaintiffs appealed.

HELD: (HL) The overriding question was whether the proceedings were an abuse of the court. There could not be a rigid distinction between public and private law. The Director General was performing public duties, but the dispute was essentially over the terms of a contract, to which the originating summons procedure was appropriate. The appeal would be allowed. [1996] 1 W.L.R. 48

COMMENTARY
This case represents a further move, evidenced in *Roy v. Kensington and Chelsea and Westminister Family Practitioner Committee*, away from a rigid approach to the public-private law divide towards a more pragmatic approach to procedure.

Nature of the body whose decisions are to be reviewed

KEY PRINCIPLE: *In considering whether the matter was a public law one the court must take into account not only the source of a body's powers and duties but also their nature.*

R. v. Panel on Takeovers and Mergers, ex p. Datafin Plc

The panel was the City's self-regulating mechanism for dealing with takeovers and mergers. The applicants complained about the conduct of their competitors in a take-over bid. They were refused leave to seek judicial review of the panel's decision to reject their complaint and appealed.

HELD: (CA) Although the panel purported to be part of a system of self-regulation and to derive its power solely from the consent of those whom its decisions affected, it was in fact operating as an integral part of a governmental framework for regulating the City. It was under a duty to act judicially and was open to judicial review. However, on the facts there were no grounds for interfering with its decision. [1987] 1 Q.B. 815

COMMENTARY
English law does not offer a clear definition of what is a public body so this case is an important illustration of what the courts mean when applying the criterion of exercising a public function. There are two aspects to the definition: first the Panel's decisions were clearly seen by the Government to be part of its regulation of the City; and secondly those affected had no choice but to submit to its jurisdiction.

KEY PRINCIPLE: *Judicial review is not available against domestic tribunals whose authority derives from contract.*

Law v. National Greyhound Racing Club Ltd

The plaintiff, a greyhound trainer, had his licence to practice suspended for six months by the club, the sport's regulatory body. He brought an action by originating summons for a declaration that the decision to suspend him was unreasonable and unfair and thus a breach of his contract with the club. The club applied to have the proceedings struck out on the basis that they should have been brought under R.S.C., Ord. 53. The judge dismissed the application and the club appealed.

HELD: (QB) The club's authority to suspend the trainer's licence was derived from his contract with the club. Although its decisions might affect the public, the club was a domestic tribunal whose decisions were not open to judicial review. The action had been brought in the proper forum and would not be struck out. [1983] 1 W.L.R. 1302

COMMENTARY
Some commentators have suggested that bodies which exercise monopolistic powers should be subject to judicial review because in such instances people have no choice but to submit to their jurisdiction. It was held here however, that although the Jockey Club regulated racing it was not part of a Government regulatory scheme. In a number of similar cases involving sporting bodies it has been held that judicial review is not appropriate where a body exercises consensual jurisdiction.

R. v. Fernhill Manor School, ex p. A

A girl expelled from an independent school for alleged bullying had no opportunity to answer the allegations. She sought judicial review, claiming a breach of natural justice.

HELD: The rules of natural justice had not been followed, but the case fell into the private sector in which public law remedies could not provide relief. Public law remedies were not available where the legal relationship was based on contract rather than the exercise of a power derived from statute [1993] 1 F.L.R. 620.

COMMENTARY
A public law element does not arise simply because the action complained of is taken by a public body. Thus a senior nursing officer was denied judicial review of his dismissal by a health authority because infringement of his contract of employment

was a private law matter, even though the authority was a creature of statute (*R. v. East Berkshire Health Authority, ex p. Walsh* [1985] Q.B. 152). But a prison officer dismissed contrary to natural justice for alleged breach of a statutory code of conduct was entitled to judicial review of the decision (*R. v. Secretary of State for the Home Department, ex p. Benwell* [1985] Q.B. 554).

KEY PRINCIPLE: *Decisions of officers of a nature where legislation would not encroach were not suitable for review.*

R. v. Chief Rabbi of the United Hebrew Congregations of Great Britain and the Commonwealth, ex p. Wachmann

The applicant sought judicial review of a decision by the Chief Rabbi declaring him unfit to act as an orthodox rabbi.

HELD: (QB) For a decision of a non-governmental body to be subject to the court's supervisory jurisdiction there had potentially to be a governmental interest in the decision-making power, in that the body was exercising, as part of a self-regulatory system, control over an activity which might otherwise be subject to statutory regulation. Parliament would not seek to control the Chief Rabbi's regulatory responsibilities should he abdicate them, as they were essentially religious functions [1992] 1 W.L.R. 1036

COMMENTARY
This marks an extension of the *Datafin* (see page 65) analysis in holding that for the decision of a body not established by statute or prerogative to a be a public law matter there had to be government not merely a public interest in the matter. Here the Government would not exercise the functions of the Chief Rabbi if he failed to do so since these were spiritual.

No alternative remedy

KEY PRINCIPLE: *Judicial review is not normally available where there is an alternative remedy.*

R. v. Chief Constable of the Merseyside Police, ex p. Calveley

Complaints were made against five police officers but the chief constable allowed two years to go by before giving formal

notice of the complaints as required by regulations. At a
disciplinary hearing the chief constable rejected a submission
that the officers had been prejudiced by the delay because
their notes and logs relating to the matters complained of had
been routinely destroyed. The officers were found guilty and
dismissed from the force. They gave notice of appeal under
the police discipline regulations and also sought judicial
review. The Divisional Court refused to hear the judicial
review application before the disciplinary appeal. The officers
appealed.

HELD: (CA) Judicial review would be available only in excep-
tional circumstances where there was an alternative remedy by
way of appeal. Where the basis of the application was delay,
judicial review should only be granted if the delay amounted to
an abuse of process. In this case, the delay had been a serious
departure from the disciplinary process which justified the
grant of judicial review. Judicial review should not be granted
merely because it was more effective and convenient than the
alternative appeal route. [1986] 1 Q.B. 424.

KEY PRINCIPLE: *Remedies are discretionary and may not
be available even where grounds for review are found.*

Glynn v. Keele University

A number of students were seen naked in the university pre-
cincts. The Vice-Chancellor, without hearing the student, pun-
ished one with a £10 fine and exclusion from the residence for
the following academic year. The student was informed that he
had a right of appeal, but when notice of the appeal hearing
arrived he was abroad and on his return found that the appeal
had been dismissed in his absence. Instead of asking for a
rehearing, he issued a writ and sought an injunction restraining
the university from excluding him from residence.

HELD: The Vice-Chancellor was acting in a quasi-judicial
capacity in exercising his powers under the university statutes.
The plaintiff had failed to make arrangements which would
have enabled him to attend an appeal hearing and had not
applied for a re-hearing of his case. There was a discretion in
the court to grant an injunction where natural justice had

failed. But although the plaintiff would lose the opportunity of making a plea in mitigation, the court would not do so in this case because the offence merited a severe penalty. [1971] 1 W.L.R. 487

7. JUDICIAL REVIEW GROUNDS—ILLEGALITY

KEY PRINCIPLE: *The grounds for review which already applied to powers under statute could be summarised as illegality, irrationality and procedural impropriety.*

Council for Civil Service Unions v. Minister for the Civil Service

For facts see page 29.

HELD: (HL) The grounds for judicial review of administrative action could be classified under three heads: illegality, irrationality and procedural impropriety. Others, including perhaps proportionality, might be added later (*per* Lord Diplock). [1985] 1 A.C. 374

COMMENTARY

Lord Diplock considered that a further development on a case-by-case basis may in the course of time add further grounds. Over the years the courts have developed an elaborate body of principles to be applied to judicial review of actions and omissions of administrators. However, there is no general agreement on a classification of grounds and de Smith has said "the task of separating them analytically in particular fact situations may be almost insuperable." The three fold classification is itself subject to varying subdivisions and not all commentators agree on the nomenclature.

Substantive Ultra Vires

KEY PRINCIPLE: *For a public body to take a decision or to embark upon a decision-making process without authority or power means that it acts ultra vires or without jurisdiction.*

R. v. Secretary of State for the Home Department, ex p. Leech (No. 2)

A prisoner who was involved in various civil actions feared his correspondence with his solicitor was being censored under Prison Rules. He applied for judicial review to quash the governor's power of censorship over letters between himself and his legal adviser as being *ultra vires* the Prison Act. The application was refused at first instance and the prisoner appealed.

HELD: (CA) A convicted prisoner retained all civil rights which were not removed either expressly or by necessary implication. The Prison Act authorised some interference with the right of confidentiality. But it was a fundamental principle that every citizen had a right of unimpeded access to a court and to a solicitor for receiving advice and assistance in that connection. Prison staff could read correspondence between prisoner and solicitor to see that it was bona fide. But for the prison to stop prisoner-solicitor correspondence under prison rule 33(3) on the ground that its contents were of inordinate length was *ultra vires*. [1994] Q.B. 198

Error of Law

KEY PRINCIPLE: *All errors of law are ultra vires in that the tribunal has exceeded its rightful jurisdiction.*

Anisminic v. Foreign Compensation Commission

The Foreign Compensation Act 1950 provided that the determination of the Foreign Compensation Commission of any application made to them under the Act should not be called in question in any court of law. The owners of property sequestrated by the Egyptian government following the Anglo-French-Israeli invasion in 1956 claimed they were entitled to compensation but the commission provisionally found against their claim. The owners sought a declaration that the commission had misconstrued an Order in Council made under the Act, but the commission claimed the court had no jurisdiction. The owners lost in the Court of Appeal but appealed to the House of Lords.

HELD: (HL) A determination did not include everything which purported to be a determination but not in fact a determination because the commission had misconstrued the Order which defined their jurisdiction. The court could consider whether or not the commission's finding was a nullity. It was a nullity and the owners were entitled to the declaration they sought. [1969] 2 A.C. 147

COMMENTARY
The House of Lords here made virtually obsolete the distinction between errors of law which went to jurisdiction and those within jurisdiction. It held that all errors of law went to jurisdiction even where they were errors made in actually exercising the power rather than errors in establishing whether the power existed. The Foreign Compensation Commission had asked themselves a question they were not empowered to ask, namely the nationality of the successor in title, and had hereby made an error of law which took them outside their jurisdiction. This was a controversial decision because of the existence of an ouster clause in the legislation whereby Parliament had precluded review of findings of the Commission. Here the purported decision was in fact a nullity since it was made outside jurisdiction therefore review was possible. On ouster clauses and time limits see *R. v. Secretary of State for Environment, ex p. Ostler* [1977] Q.B. 122.

R. v. Lord President of the Privy Council, ex p. Page
A Hull University staff member was appointed on the basis that he could not be removed without good cause before the retirement age of 67. He was made redundant and petitioned the university's Visitor (the Lord President) for a declaration that the university's decision to make him redundant was *ultra vires* the university's powers and thus invalid. The Visitor rejected the petition and the Divisional Court granted the applicant the declaration he sought. On appeal by the university the Court of Appeal held the Visitor's decision to be open to judicial review but decided the university had not exceeded its powers. Both sides appealed.

HELD: (HL) The Divisional Court had no jurisdiction to hear the judicial review application because the Visitor's decision was not reviewable for error of fact or law in the adjudication of the dispute between the staff member and the university. Judicial review would have been available had the Visitor acted outside his jurisdiction in the sense that he did not have the power to enter into the adjudication of the dispute, or had abused his power or had acted contrary to natural justice. In any event the Visitor's decision had been correct. [1993] A.C. 682

COMMENTARY
Although review was denied in this case the House of Lords reaffirmed the position in *Anisminic* that all errors of law went to jurisdiction. The older view was that there could exist what was known as "an error of law on the face of the record" which arises when a body is acting within its powers but errs in law while doing so and that error appears on the face of the record of that decision. Such an error, *i.e.* one *intra vires*, is reviewable under the inherent jurisdiction of the court to control all inferior tribunals. All errors of law are now jurisdictional.

Error of Fact

KEY PRINCIPLE: *An error of fact can be reviewable if the error is jurisdictional. This will occur where the existence of a particular state of affairs is a condition precedent to the tribunal, having jurisdiction.*

Khawaja v. Home Secretary
Two immigrants, Khera and Khawaja, had each been given leave to enter the United Kingdom. Khera had married after being given leave but before coming to Britain, so that the authorities were unaware of his marriage when he came into the country. When his wife applied to join him, he was arrested and faced deportation. Khawaja had married after obtaining his visa to enter the United Kingdom and he and his wife had entered the country separately. He claimed on arrival that he was visiting a cousin. He had also lied about the date of his marriage. Both men sought judicial review and the cases were heard together. Their applications for judicial review were both dismissed by the Divisional Court and the Court of Appeal.

HELD: (HL) An "illegal entrant" under the Immigration Act 1971 included anyone who had obtained leave to enter by fraud or deception. It was not limited to clandestine entrants. The court had to decide on an application for judicial review of an immigration officer's decision to detain any person in the United Kingdom as an illegal entrant whether there had been sufficient evidence to justify the officer's belief. The court's duty was not limited to inquiring whether there was some evidence on which the officer had been entitled to decide as he had. The presence of sufficient evidence was a precedent fact of which the reviewing court had to be satisfied. Silence could amount to deception but there was no duty of candour on immigrants. Khera would be granted judicial review, Khawaja refused. [1984] A.C. 74

COMMENTARY

The essence of a jurisdictional matter is that it is not concerned with the actual decision but with a collateral question. Such decisions are preliminary matters which can be challenged by judicial review even in those cases where the statute has precluded review of the final decision itself. This case is an example of the no evidence principle which has been developed as part of the error of jurisdictional fact doctrine. In this case the court was reluctant to allow the determination of fact on such a sensitive issue to be left to an official acting alone. By contrast In *R. v. Hillingdon L.B.C., ex p. Pulhofer* [1986] 1 All E.R. 467, the House of Lords left the determination of the meaning of "accommodation" under section 7 of the Housing (Homeless Persons) Act 1977 to the local authority.

Abuse of Discretion

Administrators frequently are given discretion to act as opposed to a duty to act where action is mandatory. The following cases illustrate how the courts have tried to structure the exercise of such discretion.

Improper Purpose

KEY PRINCIPLE: *Administrators must not exercise their discretion for an improper purpose.*

Wheeler v. Leicester City Council

Three members of the Leicester rugby team were selected to play for England on a tour of South Africa. The team used a ground belonging to the council. The council questioned the club as to whether it would press the players not to take part in the tour. The club replied that it was a matter for the players whether they went on the tour, but that the club had supplied them with material explaining the case against sporting links with South Africa. After the tour, in which the three players participated, the council banned the club for a year from using the ground. An application by club members for judicial review was refused and the applicants appealed. The Court of Appeal by a majority dismissed the appeal and held that the council was entitled, when exercising its discretionary powers, to have regard to the need to promote good race relations. The club members appealed.

HELD: (HL) The council had power to consider the best interests of race relations when exercising its discretion to manage the ground. But in the absence of any unlawful or improper conduct by the club, the ban was unreasonable and a breach of the council's duty to act fairly. The council's actions were a procedural impropriety and a misuse of its statutory powers. [1985] A.C. 1054

Roberts v. Hopwood

The Public Health Act 1875 empowered Metropolitan Borough Councils to pay their employees "such . . . wages as [the council] may think fit". Poplar Borough Council paid £4 a week to its lowest paid employees, despite a dramatic fall in the cost of living, because it believed this to be the least a local authority should pay to adult workers. The district auditor found that the payments were not wages but gratuities to the employees. Starting with the pre-war rate of wages, he added on a cost of living bonus and a further £1 as margin and surcharged the councillors for the rest. The Divisional Court upheld the surcharge, but it was overturned in the Court of Appeal. The district auditor appealed.

HELD: (HL) The council's statutory discretion must be exercised reasonably. The fixing of wages without regard to existing labour conditions was not a proper exercise of the discretion. An expenditure on a lawful object might be so excessive as to be unlawful. The disallowance and surcharge would be upheld. [1925] A.C. 578

COMMENTARY
These cases illustrate the difficulties of defining grounds; both could also be considered as examples of irrationality (see page 80).

Padfield v. Minister of Agriculture, Fisheries and Food

The Milk Marketing Board fixed prices at which producers had to sell their milk. Under the Agricultural Marketing Act 1958 different prices were fixed in each of the board's eleven regions, to reflect variations in transport costs between the regions. The same price differentials had been in operation for several years though transport costs had altered. South-east region produmanagement cers wanted to change the differentials, but were unable to get a majority of the national board to agree. They asked the minister to mount an inquiry under the Act but he refused. The producers applied for an order of mandamus to compel the minister to appoint the inquiry.

HELD: (HL) The minister's discretion had been conferred by Parliament so that it could be used to promote the policy and objects of the Act, which were for the court to determine as a matter of law. The minister's discretion was not unlimited and the court was entitled to interfere if it appeared that the effect of his refusal to intervene was to frustrate the purpose of the Act. The order sought would be made. [1968] A.C. 997

COMMENTARY

One reason for the minister's failure to refer the complaint was that publicity might be politically damaging. This could also be seen as taking into account an irrelevant consideration (see page 79).

Congreve v. Home Office

The Home Secretary increased television licence fees from £12 to £18 with effect from April 1 and instructed Post Office counter clerks not to renew licences for the period after the date the rise came into force until the rise was in force. The applicant sought in March to renew his licence which expired on March 31. The counter clerk in violation of the instruction issued him with a new licence at the old £12 rate. The Home Office wrote to him saying that the licence would be revoked unless he paid the extra £6. He sought a declaration that the threatened revocation would be unlawful, invalid and of no effect. The judge refused the declaration and he appealed.

HELD: (CA) The courts would stop the Home Secretary exercising his statutory discretion arbitrarily or improperly.

The applicant's licence was valid when issued and there was nothing in the legislation to prevent the holding of overlapping licences. The minister had acted unlawfully in excess of his authority. [1976] 1 Q.B. 629

COMMENTARY
The minister wished to revoke the licences to avoid loss of revenue which was an improper purpose since it could be implied that power to revoke was restricted to illegal licences.

Fettering of Discretion

KEY PRINCIPLE: *The decision maker can adopt a policy legitimately but in exercising it must not exclude the merits of individual cases and prevent the authority from exercising its discretion in individual cases.*

Lavender & Son Ltd v. Minister of Housing and Local Government

A gravel extraction company bought some land part of which was in an area reserved for agriculture and sought planning permission to work the site. The Ministry of Agriculture told the planning authority it had strong objections on agricultural grounds. The planning authority had no objection on amenity or highway grounds, but refused permission on grounds of prematurity and because of the Minister of Agriculture's objections. The company appealed under the Town and Country Planning Act 1962 to the Minister of Housing whose inspector concluded the land could be properly restored after extraction, but would made no recommendation because he was in no position to judge whether the reservation for agricultural use should be maintained. The Minister refused planning permission and told the application that it was his policy not to release land for working "unless the Minister of Agriculture is not opposed to working".

HELD: (DC) The Minister was obliged to exercise his statutory discretion by giving consideration to whether on planning grounds the land could be worked. By his stated policy he had in effect inhibited himself from exercising his discretion in cases where the Minister of Agriculture had raised objection. The Minister had wrongly delegated his statutory duty to the Minister of Agriculture. [1970] 1 W.L.R. 1231

British Oxygen Co Ltd v. Minister of Technology

The company produced gases which were various transported in small or large road tankers, in hydrogen trailers towed by tractors or in metal cylinders. It sought industrial development grants for new transporters but the Board of Trade decided all the tankers were ineligible as "vehicles", that the hydrogen trailers and cylinders were also ineligible because they were essentially means of storage, and it would not exercise its discretion to make grants for the cylinders which cost less than £25 each. The company asked the court to determine whether the equipment was "machinery or plant" and thus eligible for grant.

HELD: (HL) The tankers and hydrogen trailers were not "machinery or plant", and thus were not eligible for grant. The cylinders might be eligible for grant, but the Minister had a discretion not to make a grant. He could adopt a policy or make a limiting rule as to the future exercise of his discretion, provided he listened to any applicant who had something new to say. The declaration was refused. [1971] A.C. 610

COMMENTARY

It is more difficult to apply this principle where an authority has to deal with a large number of applications. Lord Reid said, "What the authority must not do is to refuse to listen at all. But a Ministry or large authority may have had to deal already with a multitude of similar applications and then they will almost certainly have evolved a policy so precise that it could well be called a rule. There can be no objections to that provided the authority is always willing to listen to anyone with something new to say."

Failure to Exercise Discretion

KEY PRINCIPLE: *A public body cannot undertake by contract or some other form of agreement not to exercise a discretionary power.*

Ayr Harbour Trustees v. Oswald

Harbour trustees were empowered by Parliament to take land necessary for their undertaking. The respondent's land was to be taken and compensation assessed by an arbiter. Before the arbiter decided, the trustees lodged a minute stating that the conveyance should restrict their use of the land so as to allow continued access by the respondent to the harbour. The arbiter found £4,900 payable for unrestricted use by the trustees, but only £2,786 if the trustees' use was restricted. The respondent wanted the full compensation.

HELD: (HL) Under their special Act of Parliament, the trustees had power at any time to build on the land and destroy the respondent's access to the harbour. In any event the trustees were not competent to dispense with the future exercise of their powers. Full compensation would be paid. [1883] 8 A.C. 623

COMMENTARY

The covenant the trustees sought to make was *ultra vires*. Parliament had to be assumed to have conferred the powers of compulsory purchase on the grounds that it would be for the public good. An authority cannot bind itself not to use those powers.

Improper Delegation

KEY PRINCIPLE: *When a statute has delegated a function to an administrative authority it cannot delegate that function to another body.*

R. v. Director of Public Prosecutions, ex p. Association of First Division Civil Servants

The DPP began using non-lawyers to review certain categories of case in order to decide whether the evidence was sufficient to prosecute and whether the prosecution was in the public interest. The First Division Association sought judicial review.

HELD: (DC) Such a decision could not lawfully be delegated to an unqualified person because one the main purposes of the Prosecution of Offences Act 1985 which established an independent Crown Prosecution Service was to bring a legal mind to bear on each prosecution. *The Times*, May 24, 1988

Carltona Ltd v. Commissioners of Works

A food factory was requisitioned under defence regulations. The owners challenged the requisition decision because it gave a reason not mentioned in the regulation and the requisitioning authority had not brought their minds to bear on the question, and had they done so could not possibly have concluded as they did.

HELD: (CA) Parliament had given the executive the discretion to decide when a requisition order should be made under the regulation. No court could interfere with that discretion if exercised properly. [1943] 2 All E.R. 560

COMMENTARY

The court here accepted that except for those occasions where statute expressly demands that a Minister acts personally his powers are going to be exercised on his behalf by senior civil servants. Lord Green M.R. stated: "The whole system of departmental organisation and administration is based on the view that Ministers being responsible to Parliament will see that important duties are committed to experienced officials. If they do not do that Parliament is the place where complaints must be made against them." In *R. v. Secretary of State for the Home Office, ex p. Oladehinde* [1991] 1 A.C. 254 the House of Lords held that often when a civil servant takes action he is acting as the *alter ego* of a minister and there is no delegation.

Irrelevant Considerations

KEY PRINCIPLE: *If a public body takes an irrelevant consideration into account or fails to take note of a relevant consideration in making a decision the decision will be ultra vires.*

Bromley London Borough Council v. Greater London Council

The Greater London Council voted to implement the "fares fair" policy, levying a supplementary rate to subsidise public transport by reducing fares. Bromley Council was refused judicial review of the GLC decision, but the decision was reversed in the Court of Appeal. The GLC appealed.

HELD: (HL) The GLC owed a fiduciary duty to ratepayers to have regard to their interests and were under a statutory obligation to apply business principles to the conduct of public transport and had acted *ultra vires* the relevant legislation and in breach of its fiduciary duty. [1983] 1 A.C. 768

COMMENTARY
This case could also be seen as one decided on grounds of fettering of discretion since the GLC had (*per* Lord Diplock) regarded itself as irrevocably committed to carry out the reduction in fares whatever the cost to rate payers because that was in the election manifesto of the majority party.

R. v. Somerset County Council, ex p. Fewings

Land held for amenity purposes by the council in the Quantock Hills was part of an area of outstanding natural beauty. The council voted to ban stag-hunting over the land. Representatives of the Quantock Staghounds sought judicial review. The judge held that the majority of the council had voted because of moral repugnance to hunting which was not relevant to the exercise of the powers under the Local Government Act 1972 which they claimed to be exercising in imposing the ban. The council appealed.

HELD: (CA) The council had failed to take account of the objects of the statute under which they claimed to be acting. As local authority landowners as opposed to private landowners they were subject to an overriding statutory constraint. They had not exercised their power to promote the benefit of the area and had not been entitled to make their decision on the ground relied on. [1995] 1 W.L.R. 1037

COMMENTARY
The court's view was that the Council's opinion of the cruelty of stag hunting although not necessarily an irrelevant consideration was only one of the factors which should be considered.

8. JUDICIAL REVIEW GROUNDS—IRRATIONALITY

KEY PRINCIPLE: *A decision maker in whom a discretionary power is vested must not exercise that power in a way that no reasonable body would.*

Associated Provincial Picture Houses Ltd v. Wednesbury Corporation

The Sunday Entertainments Act 1932 empowered local authorities to licence Sunday cinema opening "subject to such conditions as the authority may think fit to impose". The corporation granted a Sunday licence to the company on condition that nobody under the age of 15 was admitted. The company sought judicial review.

HELD: (CA) The local authority had not acted unreasonably or *ultra vires*. The court was only entitled to review the exercise of so unlimited a power with a view to seeing whether the authority had taken account of matters it ought not to have taken into account, or disregarded matters it should have taken into account. [1948] 1 K.B. 223

COMMENTARY

Lord Green said that taking irrelevant considerations into account and exercising a discretionary power for an improper purpose would constitute unreasonable actions (see Chapter seven). However, unreasonableness is also in itself an invalidating factor. Apart from irrelevant considerations and improper purpose Lord Green said that "if a decision on a competent matter is so unreasonable that no reasonable authority could ever come to it then the courts can interfere" but this would require "something overwhelming". According to Lord Green irrationality is a comprehensive term so it does cover behaviour which might also be described as illegal. In *Council for Civil Service Unions v. Minister for the Civil Service (GCHQ case)* (see page 29) Lord Diplock had in contrast confined the term "irrationality" to the rather extreme cases and used the term "illegality" to conduct which has in other cases been called unreasonable.

In practice it is difficult to challenge a decision on grounds of unreasonableness alone. Where an applicant succeeds it is usually in connection with improper purpose and/or irrelevant considerations. This category comes closest to challenging the merits of a decision and it might be felt that if it were a straightforward road to success the court was vetoing powers conferred by Parliament on public authorities and substituting its own view for that of the authority to which discretion was given.

Wheeler v. Leicester City Council
(For facts see page 73.)

HELD: (HL) The council had a statutory power to consider the best interests of race relations when managing the ground, but in the absence of any unlawful or improper conduct by the club, the 12-month ban was unreasonable and a breach of the council's duty to act fairly. The council's actions were a procedural impropriety and the ban would be quashed. [1985] A.C. 1054

COMMENTARY
The Court of Appeal and the House of Lords found different applications of the irrationality principle. In the Court of Appeal Ackner L.J. considered the council's decision was not one that no reasonable local authority could have taken, however in the House of Lords, Lord Roskill considered the council's decision was within *Wednesbury* unreasonableness in that it had applied pressure beyond persuasion. This case can be considered under a number of heads including improper purpose and taking irrelevant considerations into account.

KEY PRINCIPLE: *In its application to local authority decisions the Wednesbury test means that the decision maker must have acted with manifest absurdity.*

Secretary of State for Education v. Tameside Metropolitan Borough Council

A Labour local education authority proposed to introduce comprehensive secondary schooling. Its plans were approved by the Secretary of State for implementation in September 1976. The matter was an issue in local elections which were won by the Conservative opposition. The new administrative body changed the plans so as to retain three grammar schools which would have gone comprehensive. The Secretary of State directed the authority to carry out the original plan as to change it would be too disruptive and obtained a writ of mandamus to that effect in the Divisional Court. The order was overturned on appeal and the Secretary of State appealed.

HELD: (HL) The Secretary of State was not entitled to require the authority to abandon their policy because he disagreed with it. He could give a direction only if the authority were acting unreasonably in what they were entitled to do. There had been no proper ground for intervention against the change of plan. [1977] A.C. 1014

R. v. Secretary of State for the Environment, ex p. Hammersmith and Fulham London Borough Council

The Secretary of State acting applied the Local Government Finance Act 1988 to impose limits on the amount of Community Charge which could be levied by designated councils. Twenty-one councils were designated, and 19 sought judicial review of the decision to designate, on the grounds that the Secretary of State had failed to have regard to the individual spending needs of the individual authorities and had designated only those authorities with high standard spending assessments. Judicial review was refused in the Divisional Court and in the Court of Appeal. The councils appealed.

HELD: (HL) The Secretary of State's decision to designate particular authorities was based on principles of general application as to what as a matter of political opinion constituted excessive spending. The application of those principles only to authorities with high standard spending assessments did not contravene the legislation. The authorities had no legitimate expectation that the Secretary of State would only prevent them spending above what any reasonable authority would incur. The Secretary of State's powers under the Act involved the exercise of a political judgment which was not open to challenge on grounds of irrationality short of bad faith, improper motive or manifest absurdity. [1991] 1 A.C. 521

COMMENTARY

The council had applied on grounds of illegality, irrationality and procedural impropriety. The House of Lords showed concern that the courts would not be embroiled in the political arena in deciding that the Secretary of State's decision involved the exercise of political judgement which was subject to approval by the House of Commons. The two cases above confirm that the courts take the view that to be unreasonable there must be a decision which no reasonable authority could take. The test is not what the court considers reasonable. By contrast in *R. v. Secretary of State for Defence, ex p. Smith*

[1996] Q.B. 517 the Court of Appeal suggested that in cases involving individual liberties a less stringent test would be applied. However, in that case involving a ban on homosexuals in the forces the Ministry's decision was not irrational since the policy was supported by both Houses of Parliament and by those whose professional advice had been sought.

9. PROCEDURAL IMPROPRIETY, OTHER GROUNDS

KEY PRINCIPLE: *The rules of natural justice have to be observed where there is a duty to act judicially and this duty is not confined to the procedure of a court of law but exists where any body of persons has legal authority (arising from statute or common law or contract) to determine questions affecting the rights (not only legal rights) of others.*

Ridge v. Baldwin

The chief constable of Brighton was tried for conspiracy to obstruct the course of justice. During the trial he was suspended from office. He was acquitted but the judge told him he had lacked the "professional and moral leadership" the public was entitled to expect. Using its powers under the Municipal Corporations Act 1882 the borough watch committee voted to dismiss him, forfeiting his pension rights. He had not been invited to appear before the committee, which confirmed its decision at a subsequent meeting at which he was represented. He sought judicial review to challenge the dismissal as a breach of natural justice.

HELD: (HL) The watch committee was in breach of the principles of natural justice as well as of the statutory regulations governing police discipline. The watch committee had three possible courses of action: dismissal, requiring the chief constable to resign or reinstating him. It was contrary to natural justice to decide the issue without hearing the chief constable. Natural justice was not confined to situations where a judicial or quasi-judicial function was being exercised. [1964] A.C. 40

COMMENTARY

This landmark decision is a recognition of the impact of decisions of administrative bodies on people's lives.

Procedural Ultra Vires

KEY PRINCIPLE: *Where Parliament has laid down a procedure which should be followed before a body can exercise its powers the body will be acting ultra vires if it does not follow the procedure.*

Agricultural Training Board v. Aylesbury Mushrooms Ltd

The Board was established under the Industrial Training Act 1964, which provided for prior consultation by the Ministry of Labour with interested organisations. Consultations were organised, in which the National Farmers Union took part, and an invitation was sent to, but not received by, a branch of the union, the Mushroom Growers Association, which was unaware that the board was being established. The Board was duly established and claimed to regulate training of mushroom growers. The Association made formal application for its members to be excluded. The Board issued a summons to determine whether the Minister had complied with his duty of consultation before making the order establishing the Board, and if not, what the consequences were.

HELD: (DC) The Minister was under a duty to consult the Association. Consulting the union would have constituted consultation with its constituent parts, had not the Minister tried to consult the Association directly. Without communication and the consequent opportunity of responding, there could be no consultation. The result of the failure to consult was that the Board had no authority over mushroom growers as such. [1972] 1 W.L.R. 190

COMMENTARY

Lord Diplock in *Council of Civil Service Unions v. Minister for the Civil Service* (see page 29)recognised two aspects to procedural impropriety, first, failure to observe procedures laid down in the relevant statute and secondly, failure to follow the common law principles of natural justice. Specified procedural requirement may fall into two sorts, mandatory or directory. However, it is not always possible to distinguish them and a minor breach of a mandatory requirement will not necessarily be significant.

Natural Justice

KEY PRINCIPLE: *A person cannot incur the loss of liberty, property or livelihood unless he has an opportunity of a fair hearing.*

Cooper v. Wandsworth Board of Works

Under the Metropolis Local Management Act 1855 the Board of Works had power to alter or demolish a house where the builder had neglected to give notice of his intention to build seven days before proceeding to lay or dig the foundations. The plaintiff had given only five days' notice before starting to build. The house was already built up to the second storey when late one evening council workers came and razed it to the ground. The builder brought an action in damages for the house, claiming that the Board had improperly exercised its power by acting without notice and failing to give him an opportunity to be heard.

HELD: (CCP) A person could not be deprived of his property without a hearing. The council's statutory power to demolish did not empower them to do so without giving the builder an opportunity of being heard. (1863) 14 C.B. (N.S.) 180

KEY PRINCIPLE: *The content of a right to a hearing may vary according to the circumstances of the case.*

McInnis v. Onslow-Fane

The plaintiff applied for a boxing manager's licence but was refused without an oral hearing. The boxing board of control gave him no reasons for refusal. He sought a declaration that the board had acted in breach of natural justice and unfairly.

HELD: (QB) The court was entitled to intervene to ensure natural justice. But the case did not involve an existing right, nor had the plaintiff any legitimate expectation of success. The board was under a duty to reach an honest conclusion without bias but was under no obligation to give reasons, nor to grant an oral hearing. The application would be dismissed. [1978] 1 W.L.R. 1520

KEY PRINCIPLE: *No man can be a judge in his own cause.*

Dimes v. Grand Junction Canal Co.

A dispute over the ownership of part of the Grand Junction Canal led the canal company to apply for an injunction before the Vice-Chancellor against a landowner who was obstructing navigation. The injunction was granted and on appeal the Lord Chancellor confirmed it. It later emerged that the Lord Chancellor held shares in the company worth several thousand pounds. The landowner appealed to the House of Lords.

HELD: (HL) The appeal would be allowed. Because of his interest, the Lord Chancellor was disqualified from sitting as a judge in the case and his decision was thus voidable and must be reversed. Despite his disqualification, the Lord Chancellor was still competent to grant leave to appeal to the House of Lords in the case. [1852] 3 H.L. Cas. 759

COMMENTARY

This is the leading case on matters involving possible bias arising out of a pecuniary interest. The Lord Chancellor could not have been supposed to have been influenced by his interest in the company but it was important that the rule that no one should be a judge in his own cause should be seen to be upheld.

R. v. Gough

The defendant was convicted of conspiring with his brother to commit robbery. The brother had been discharged at the committal stage but after the defendant had been convicted and sentenced made a scene in court and was recognised by one of the jury as her next door neighbour. The defence raised with the judge the possibility of bias but he held he was *functus officio*. The Court of Appeal dismissed the defendant's appeal and he appealed to the House of Lords.

HELD: (HL) The test to be applied in all cases of apparent bias was whether in all the circumstances of the case there appeared to be a real danger of bias such that justice required the decision should not stand. The only category of case where bias would be assumed was where the tribunal had a pecuniary or proprietary interest in the subject-matter of the proceedings. The appeal would be dismissed. [1993] A.C. 646

COMMENTARY
In cases such as these involving non-pecuniary interest the words "real danger" should be taken to denote a possibility not a probability.

R. v. Inner West London Coroner, ex p. Dallaglio

Two mothers who had lost children when the Marchioness pleasure boat sank after a collision in the Thames became involved in a dispute with the coroner while the inquest was adjourned pending the outcome of criminal proceedings. One of the mothers applied unsuccessfully for an exhumation order, having been denied an opportunity to see her son's body. She believed the hands had been cut off her son's body for identification purposes. The coroner expressed a belief that she had been psychologically affected by grief and was not acting rationally. The two mothers took the story to a newspaper and the coroner met journalists in an attempt to set the record straight. In the course of that meeting he described one of the women as "unhinged" and displayed hostility to her. The coroner later wrote to the relatives of all the victims asking whether they wanted the inquest reconvened. He subsequently refused to remove himself on grounds of bias or to resume the inquests, on the grounds that only a minority of families wanted resumption. An application by the mothers for judicial review was refused in the Divisional Court and they appealed.

HELD: (CA) Where there was a challenge to a court for bias, and the court expressly disavowed any suggestion of actual bias, it was necessary to consider whether there was a real danger that the decision-maker was unconsciously biased. The applicant had to demonstrate not that there was a real possibility that the coroner's decision would have been different but for the bias, but that the real danger of bias had affected the decision. The coroner's use of the word "unhinged" indicated a real possibility that the coroner had unconsciously become biased and the inquest should be resumed before a different coroner. [1994] 4 All E.R. 139

KEY PRINCIPLE: *The duty to act fairly applies to a prison governor when exercising disciplinary functions.*

Leech v. Parkhurst Prison deputy governor

A prisoner was penalised for a disciplinary offence. The proceedings were carried out in breach of natural justice but the prison authorities claimed the Secretary of State had no power to quash the guilty finding. The application was refused in the Divisional Court, but leave to appeal was granted by the Court of Appeal, which rejected judicial review on the sole ground that it was bound by *R. v. Deputy Governor of Camphill Prison, ex p. King* [1985] Q.B. 735.

HELD: (HL) An essential characteristic of the rights of the subject, even in prison, was a right of recourse to the courts unless some statute provided otherwise. No provision in the Prison Act 1952 derogated from that principle in relation to the governor's exercise of disciplinary powers. The adjudication would be quashed and *R. v. Deputy Governor of Camphill Prison, ex p. King* [1985] Q.B. 735 overruled. [1988] A.C. 533

KEY PRINCIPLE: *Availability of legal representation is a matter of discretion.*

R. v. Board of Visitors of H.M. Prison, the Maze, ex p. Hone

A prisoner facing disciplinary proceedings before the Board of Visitors was refused legal representation and sought judicial review.

HELD: (HL) Natural justice did not automatically require that a prisoner facing disciplinary proceedings be legally represented. The application would be rejected. [1988] A.C. 379

COMMENTARY

This case emphasises the flexibility of the application of the principles of natural justice. A Board of Visitors should exercise its discretion to allow legal representation if the nature, complexity and seriousness of the offence and the nature of the penalty require it. Furthermore, in exercising discretion whether to allow legal representation the Board of Visitors must not fetter themselves for example by adopting a policy that legal representation would never be allowed. Each case must be looked at on its merits.

KEY PRINCIPLE: *Hearings before prison governors should be conducted in accordance with the principles of natural justice and this may require allowing witnesses to be called and hearsay evidence to be excluded.*

R. v. Hull Prison Board of Visitors, ex p. St. Germain (No. 2)

Prison visitors hearing disciplinary proceedings against prisoners following a riot refused to allow certain witnesses to be called on behalf of the prisoners and admitted statements by prison officers who were not called to give evidence. The Divisional Court refused judicial review, but that decision was reversed in the Court of Appeal and the matter was remitted to the Divisional Court for hearing and determination.

Held: (DC) Most of the applications would be granted for unfairness in refusing to exercise the discretion to allow witnesses to be called and to refuse to admit hearsay evidence. [1979] 3 All E.R. 545

COMMENTARY
The duty to act fairly can be applied in a range of contexts and does not necessarily mean that a judicial process should be adopted. Compare *R. v. Commissioner for Racial Equality, ex p. Cottrell & Rothon* [1980] 1 W.L.R. 1580 where the Court of Appeal held that the Commission was under no obligation to provide an opportunity for cross-examination of witnesses whose evidence underpinned its decision to issue a non-discrimination notice against the applicant firm of estate agents.

KEY PRINCIPLE: *A party to any proceedings has the right to know the opposing case In advance but this does not necessarily mean a detailed case.*

R. v. Gaming Board for Great Britain, ex p. Benaim and Khaida

The applicants, French nationals, bought the Crockford's gaming club and sought a certificate of consent from the board to enable them to apply for a licence under the Gaming Act 1968. The Board heard the applicants and rejected their application, without giving reason. They complained to the Court of Appeal that they had been unfairly treated contrary to the requirements of natural justice.

HELD: (CA) The Board's statutory duty was to act fairly by giving an applicant sufficient indication of the objections to him to enable him to answer them. The Board was not obliged to disclose the sources of its information or give reasons for concluding that a certificate should be refused. [1970] 2 Q.B. 417

COMMENTARY
This case emphasises that the right to know the opposing case is not an unqualified one. An administrative body may be required to keep its sources confidential and as long as it acted with "substantial fairness" only the general nature of charges may be presented.

KEY PRINCIPLE: *There is no absolute right to an oral hearing.*

Lloyd v. McMahon

A group of Liverpool councillors were asked to make written representations as to why they should not be surcharged by the district auditor for having wilfully refused to set a rate. They did so and were surcharged. The Divisional Court dismissed their appeals on the basis that they had had sufficient opportunity to rebut the case against them. They refused to give oral evidence to the Divisional Court, whose decision was upheld by the Court of Appeal. The councillors appealed on the basis that the auditor's failure to offer an oral hearing nullified his decision.

HELD: (HL) The auditor had not acted unfairly nor had the councillors been prejudiced by the decision not to hear them. [1987] 1 A.C. 625

COMMENTARY
Per Lord Bridge, the so-called rules of natural justice are not engraved on tablets of stone.

Legitimate Expectation

The above cases illustrate how the courts have moved away from a rigid concept of procedural fairness and have developed a more flexible, pragmatic approach. One new development has been the recognition of the concept of legitimate expectation. In *GCHQ* (see page 29) Lord Roskill likened it to the right to be heard and stressed that it can take many forms. There are however, many senses to "legitimate expectation". Some of the most common are listed below.

KEY PRINCIPLE: *Where a public authority has said it will follow a certain procedure those potentially affected are entitled to a legitimate expectation that it will carry out its promise.*

Attorney-General of Hong Kong v. Ng Yuen Shiu

The applicant had entered Hong Kong illegally from Macau in 1976. Until 1980 the government had followed a "reached base" policy which allowed illegal immigrants to stay once they had reached the urban areas without being arrested. The policy was abandoned in 1980 and the government announced plans to deport illegal immigrants to China. Those who had entered from Macau made representations and it was announced that they would all be interviewed and each case considered on its merits. The applicant was detained and ordered to be removed without having the opportunity of making representations. He was refused judicial review but the appeal court granted an order of prohibition. The Attorney-General appealed.

HELD: (PC) Where a public authority promised to follow a particular procedure before making a decision, it should follow that procedure provided it was lawful. The applicant had been wrongly denied an opportunity to state his case and the removal order would be quashed. Certiorari not prohibition was the appropriate order. [1983] 2 A.C. 629

KEY PRINCIPLE: *An administrative body may create a legitimate expectation by publishing proposed procedures.*

R. v. Secretary of State for Home Department, ex p. Khan

A Home Office circular advised people who wished to adopt a child from abroad that the Home Secretary would allow a child to enter despite immigration rules provided certain specified criteria were met. The circular said the Home Secretary would in such cases check with the Department of Health whether the adopters were suitable. The applicant and his wife, who were settled in England, wished to adopt a relative's child who lived in Pakistan. The Home Office did not follow the procedure in the circular, but refused the application, applying criteria for deciding whether to admit for settlement children who were already adopted by persons settled in the United Kingdom. The applicants were refused judicial review and appealed.

HELD: (CA) The applicants had a reasonable expectation that the procedure set out in the circular would be followed. The Home Secretary had acted unfairly and unreasonably in not applying the procedure to them. Appeal allowed. [1984] 1 W.L.R. 1337

Council of Civil Service Unions v. Minister for the Civil Service (see above, page 29).

COMMENTARY

Here legitimate expectation of the right to be heard arose from a regular practice which the applicants could expect to continue. The courts have not fully resolved the question of whether there is a legitimate expectation of the right to continue to enjoy a benefit.

KEY PRINCIPLE: *A legitimate expectation of making representations may not be allowed in cases of prior misconduct.*

Cinnamond v. British Airports Authority

Six car-hire drivers had been touting for business at Heathrow airport for several years despite a string of convictions for loitering. Their prices were higher than black cab drivers, and the authority used its powers under the Airports Authority Act 1975 to tell them in writing that they would not be allowed on the airport save as bona fide passengers. The drivers were refused a declaration that the authority had acted unlawfully, and appealed.

HELD: (CA) The ban on their entry was "calculated to facilitate the discharge" of the authority's duties, and it had the power to bar them. The drivers' previous convictions deprived them of a legitimate expectation that they would be heard before the ban was imposed. [1980] 1 W.L.R. 582

Duty to Give Reasons

KEY PRINCIPLES: *Where there is a duty under statute to give reasons to an individual affected by an administrative decision the test of the adequacy of the reasons given is whether the applicant has been substantially prejudiced by the deficiency in the reason given.*

Save Britain's Heritage v. Number 1 Poultry Ltd

The owners of a group of listed buildings in the City of London proposed to build a new development on the site. The stated policy of the Secretary of State was that listed buildings capable of economic use should not be demolished. The local authority rejected the scheme but the Secretary of State held that the new building was so meritorious that it should go ahead. Objectors sought to quash the Secretary of State's decision on the grounds that he had failed to give sufficient reasons and had misdirected himself as to the effect of his policy relating to consent for demolition of listed buildings. The judge dismissed the application but the Court of Appeal found for the objectors. The owners appealed.

HELD: (HL) It was for the objectors to show that they had been prejudiced by the absence of sufficient reasons. The Secretary of State's policy was not absolute, but could be overridden in special circumstances. There had been no flaw in the decision-making process and the appeal would be allowed. [1991] 1 W.L.R. 153

KEY PRINCIPLE: *The common law may impose a duty to give reasons on administrative bodies in order to make their decisions effectively reviewable.*

R. v. Civil Service Appeal Board, ex p. Cunningham

The applicant was dismissed from his job as a prison officer. As a prison officer he was precluded from claiming unfair dismissal to an industrial tribunal, so he appealed to the Civil Service Appeal Board, which recommended reinstatement. The Home Office refused to comply with the recommendation and substituted a payment of £6,500 without indicating how the sum had been arrived at. The applicant succeeded in obtaining judicial review. The Board appealed and the applicant cross-appealed on the basis that the award was irrational.

HELD: (CA) The Board's appeal would be dismissed. The judge had correctly held that the Board was under a duty to give outline reasons for the size of award. Procedural fairness required a quasi-judicial body to give sufficient reasons to enable parties to know that it had addressed the issues and had acted lawfully. The applicant's cross-appeal would be allowed because in the absence of adequate explanations it was so far below what he could reasonably have expected as to be irrational. The case would be remitted to the Board for compensation to be reconsidered. [1992] I.C.R. 816

COMMENTARY
The Court of Appeal here acknowledged there may, in the absence of a statutory requirement, be a common law requirement for natural justice to be satisfied by the giving of outline reasons for a decision. It should, however, be noted that the Court was not creating a general duty for administrative bodies to give reasons. That may depend on the nature of the decision being given. This category overlaps with procedural impropriety.

KEY PRINCIPLE: *Procedural fairness may require a duty to give reasons.*

R. v. Secretary of State for Home Department, ex p. Doody

Four convicted murderers were told the minimum term they could expect to serve as life prisoners before being considered for parole. They sought judicial review of the Home Secretary's decision on the basis that they ought to have been consulted and that the minister could not set periods greater than those recommended by the trial judge and the Lord Chief Justice.

HELD: (HL) The Secretary of State was obliged to tell the applicants the judicial recommendations on their case and allow them an opportunity to make representations as to the term, but that the Secretary of State was not obliged to abide by the judicial recommendations, provided he gave reasons for so doing. Procedural fairness required that reasons should be given. [1994] 1 A.C. 531

COMMENTARY
Lord Mustill said that he could have come to the same decision in relation to the duty to give reasons by the reasoning made in *Cunningham*. This is now the leading case on the duty to give reasons and could be said to have indicated there was a general duty on the part of administrators to give

reasons for decisions. However in *R. v. Higher Education Funding Council, ex p. Institute of Dental Surgery* [1994] 1 W.L.R. 242 the court stressed that the requirement will depend on the circumstances of each case. There the court reviewed the law on the duty to give reasons for administrative decisions, linking it to the requirement of fairness. It identified two strands of cases: those such as *Doody* where the nature of the process itself called in fairness for reasons to be given and *Cunningham* where something peculiar to the decision or a "trigger factor" called for reasons to be given. It does not mean that differing tests of fairness should be applied. In other words the requirements of fairness will vary with the process to which they are being applied. It rejected the argument that in *Cunningham* and *Doody* it was the judicial or quasi judicial nature of the decision making that required the duty to give reasons.

Proportionality

KEY PRINCIPLE: *Proportionality is not a distinct ground of judicial review.*

R. v. Secretary of State for the Home Department, ex p. Brind

The Secretary of State made orders under the Broadcasting Act 1981 banning television and radio stations from broadcasting the words spoken by spokesmen of organisations proscribed under anti-terrorism legislation. Broadcasters sought judicial review of the orders as being outside the Secretary of State's powers among other reasons because the ban was disproportionate to its ostensible object of preventing intimidation by the organisations concerned. The application was dismissed by the Divisional Court and by the Court of Appeal. The broadcasters appealed.

HELD: (HL) The court would not apply the doctrine of proportionality because that would mean substituting its own judgment of what was needed to achieve a particular object for that of the Secretary of State who had been given that duty by Parliament. The appeal would be dismissed. [1991] 1 A.C. 696

COMMENTARY
Their Lordships had differing reasons for rejecting proportionality as a distinct ground of review. Lord Bridge agreed with

Lord Roskill that there might be scope for such a ground in the future but it was not appropriate in the present case. Lord Ackner considered it would involve a review of the merits of a decision. Lord Lowry did not see a cause for regret that proportionality was not a part of the English common law since first, Parliament entrusted discretion to elected decision makers, secondly, judges were not equipped to apply such a ground and thirdly, stability and relative certainty in administrative decisions would be jeopardised. Lord Templeman noting that the European Convention of Human Rights required proportionality to be considered said that the decision was not disproportionate to the damage which the restriction was designed to prevent but nor did it breach *Wednesbury* principles.

---

10. POLICE ACCOUNTABILITY AND POWERS

Office of Chief Constable

KEY PRINCIPLE: *The police have a duty to enforce the law but Chief Officers have a wide discretion as to the chosen means to carry out that duty. The courts will only intervene where a policy decision amounted to an abandonment of the duty.*

R. v. Metropolitan Police Commissioner, ex p. Blackburn

The police decided as a matter of policy not to enforce in London gaming clubs the statutory requirement that the games played there should not favour the banker. The applicant, a private citizen, was refused an order of mandamus to compel the police to enforce the law. He appealed, and while his appeal was pending the police announced they had changed their policy. The commissioner contended before the Court of Appeal that there was no duty to enforce the law and that since the appeal was a criminal cause or matter, the court had no jurisdiction.

HELD: (CA) The commissioner had a public duty to enforce the law, which he could be compelled to perform. Though he had a discretion not to prosecute, his discretion to make policy decisions was not absolute. The case was not a criminal cause or matter and the court had jurisdiction. [1968] 2 Q.B. 118

COMMENTARY

The distinguishing feature of this case was that the Commissioner had decided not to prosecute a whole class of offences. Judicial review lies in such an extreme case of the exercise of discretion by the police.

R. v. Chief Constable of Devon and Cornwall, ex p. Central Electricity Generating Board

The Central Electricity Generating Board was investigating the possibility of building a nuclear power station on a farm in Cornwall. The farm owners refused to allow the CEGB surveyors onto the land and pickets prevented access. The Board obtained an injunction against the farm owners and began surveying the land. There were further protests, and further injunctions were obtained against the protesters. Others took their places and prevented the Board from completing the survey, an offence under the Town and Country Planning Act 1971. The Board sought the assistance of the Chief Constable to enable it to perform its statutory duties, but the latter declined, saying a "more definitive mandate" would be needed where there was no breach of the peace and no unlawful assembly. An application for a writ of mandamus to instruct the Chief Constable to remove the protesters was dismissed in the Divisional Court and the CEGB appealed.

HELD: (CA) The police had power to remove demonstrators where there was a breach of the peace, or a reasonable apprehension that there might be a breach of the peace. The objectors were deliberately breaking the law by obstructing the survey, and the Board was entitled to use the minimum necessary force to exercise its powers. It was for the Board and the police to exercise their respective powers, but the court would not interfere by way of judicial review with the chief constable's decision not to intervene. [1982] Q.B. 458

COMMENTARY

The court was here reluctant to intervene since the chief constable was able to point to good grounds for a policy decision not to apply the law in a particular case.

Legal Basis of Police Powers

KEY PRINCIPLE: *The Crown retains a prerogative power to keep the peace.*

R. v. Secretary of State for the Home Department, ex p. Northumbria Police Authority

The Home Secretary made provisions for the supply from a central store of plastic bullets and CS gas to police forces. Chief constables could buy supplies with the approval of their police authority. But if the authority looked likely to refuse approval, the riot control equipment could be bought directly from the central store. The Northumbria police authority challenged the scheme on the grounds that the Home Secretary had no power to maintain a central store or to supply police forces without the approval of their authority, save in serious emergency. The Divisional Court held the Home Secretary had no power under the Police Act 1964 to act as he had, but could do so under the royal prerogative. Both sides appealed.

HELD: (CA) The Home Secretary was empowered by the Police Act to keep a store. Police authorities did not have an exclusive right to provide police with equipment and the Home Secretary could do so without the relevant authority's approval. The Home Secretary had authority to act at all times and not only in emergency to keep the peace. That power existed by virtue of the Police Act or in the alternative under the prerogative which existed in the Middle Ages and had never been surrendered by the Crown. [1989] 1 Q.B. 26

COMMENTARY
In this case an ancient prerogative to maintain the peace was recognised by the courts as existing alongside the statute governing police matters. The court was here demonstrating its reluctance to intervene in politically controversial areas involving police powers.

Arrest

For a valid arrest to be made it is necessary not only for there to be a power of arrest but also for the correct procedure to be followed. Powers of arrest are now codified in the Police and Criminal Evidence Act (Part 111) but to a very large extent this draws on common law principles and in addition common law powers and other specific statutory powers remain.

KEY PRINCIPLE: *Police and Criminal Evidence Act 1984, s. 28(1):*

"Subject to subsection (5) below, where a person is arrested, otherwise than by being informed that he is under arrest, the arrest is not lawful unless the person arrested is informed that he is under arrest as soon as is practicable after his arrest."

KEY PRINCIPLE: *For an arrest to be valid the fact of arrest has to be made clear and the person has to be compulsorily detained.*

Alderson v. Booth

A motorist was told by a police constable: "I shall have to ask you to come to the police station for further tests." Later he appeared before magistrates on a charge under a section of the Road Safety Act 1967 which required an arrest. The motorist told the magistrates he had gone voluntarily to the police station, and the justices decided he had not been arrested, since the words used by the constable lacked the necessary element of compulsion. The prosecutor appealed.

HELD: (DC) An arrest could be carried out by any form of words indicating compulsion. Very clear words were preferable such as "I arrest you." Whether or not the defendant had been arrested was a decision of fact for the magistrates with which the court would not interfere. [1969] 2 Q.B. 216

COMMENTARY
The importance of procedure is indicated here. Since the motorist reasonably believed that compliance with a request to accompany the officer was voluntary then an arrest had not been made. Arrest means a deprivation of liberty.

KEY PRINCIPLE: *Police and Criminal Evidence Act 1984, s. 24:*

"(4) Any person may arrest without a warrant—(a) anyone who is in the act of committing an arrestable offence; (b) anyone whom he has reasonable grounds for suspecting to be committing such an offence. (5) Where an arrestable offence has been committed, any person may arrest without a warrant—(a) anyone who is guilty of the offence; (b) anyone whom he has reasonable grounds for suspecting to be guilty of it."

R. v. Self

Two employees of a shop followed a man into the street and accused him of shoplifting. There was a scuffle in which one of the employees was scratched and kicked. A passer-by who intervened to make a citizen's arrest was also kicked. The man was acquitted of shoplifting but convicted of assault with intent to resist arrest. He appealed against conviction.

HELD: (CA) The power of arrest without warrant under section 24(5) of the Police and Criminal Evidence Act 1984 arose only when an arrestable offence had been committed. The man had been acquitted of shoplifting, so there was no offence for which he could be arrested without a warrant. He could not therefore be convicted of assault with intent to resist arrest. [1992] 1 W.L.R. 657

COMMENTARY

Clearly any citizen, including for example store detectives, who arrests under section 24(4) or (5) does so under some danger. Here the charge of resisting lawful arrest had to be dropped because the arrest itself was not lawful. The risk is also that if there is no lawful arrest the detainee may be able to sue for battery and false imprisonment.

KEY PRINCIPLE: *The reason for arrest must be made known. Police and Criminal Evidence Act, s. 28:*

"(3) Subject to subsection (5) below, no arrest is lawful unless the person arrested is informed of the ground for the arrest at the time of, or as soon as is practicable after, the arrest. (4) Where a person is arrested by a constable, subsection (3) above applies regardless of whether the ground for the arrest is obvious."

KEY PRINCIPLE: *The reason given for arrest must be the real reason.*

Christie v. Leachinsky

The plaintiff was told he was being arrested under the Liverpool Corporation Act 1921 for unlawfully possessing a bale of cloth. The police had no power to arrest for the relevant offence without warrant because the Act only allowed arrest where the person's name and address were not known. The plaintiff was tried for larceny and acquitted. He sought damages against the police for false imprisonment. The police claimed that at the time of the arrest they reasonably suspected the plaintiff of having stolen or unlawfully received the cloth.

HELD: (HL) The plaintiff had not been told the true reason for his arrest, but had been given a different reason which was not a ground for arrest without warrant. Accordingly he was entitled to damages for false imprisonment. [1947] A.C. 573

KEY PRINCIPLE: *The question whether the real reason for the arrest had been given was a question of fact.*

Abbassy v. Commissioner of Police for the Metropolis

The plaintiffs were in a car which was stopped by four police officers after being driven inconsiderately. The driver refused to satisfy one of the police officers about the ownership of the car and was arrested. The police officer gave the reason for the arrest as "unlawful possession". The passenger tried to stop the police taking the driver away and was herself arrested for obstruction and assault. Both were acquitted at trial and sued the police for assault and battery, false imprisonment and malicious prosecution. The judge ruled that the driver's arrest had been unlawful because the police officer's explanation of the arrest was insufficient. The jury found that the first plaintiff had been assaulted before arrest. The police appealed.

HELD: (CA) The judge should have left to the jury as a matter of fact the issue whether or not the police officer's explanation was sufficient. That part of the case should be retried. [1990] 1 W.L.R. 385

COMMENTARY
The police must give the reason for the arrest but that they do not have to use precise or technical language. *Christie v. Leachinsky* (see page 101) still provides clear guidance on the information which should be provided upon arrest.

KEY PRINCIPLE: *The behaviour of the arrestee may be a ground for delay in giving the reason for the arrest.*

Director of Public Prosecutions v. Hawkins

The defendant was arrested for assaulting a police officer. He struggled during the arrest, assaulting three officers. At no time was he told the reason for his arrest. He was charged with the assaults which occurred during the struggle. The magistrates accepted that there was no case to answer because the police had failed to inform the defendant of the reason for his arrest as soon as practicable so that the arrest was unlawful and the arresting officers had not been acting in the execution of their duty. The DPP appealed by way of case stated.

HELD: (DC) The police were under a duty to state the ground of arrest as soon as practicable. But they were also under a duty to maintain the arrest until the arrested person could be informed. The failure of the police after the arrest to inform the defendant of the grounds made the arrest unlawful by section 28(3) of the Police and Criminal Evidence Act 1984. However, the reason for the delay was the defendants' behaviour and at the relevant time so far as the charge was concerned it was not practicable to give the reason. The fact that the arrest had subsequently become unlawful did not retrospectively make the actions of the arresting officers unlawful. The appeal would be allowed. [1988] 1 W.L.R. 1166

COMMENTARY

The court acknowledged that the police have some leeway as to the time of informing the arrestee that he is under arrest. The lawfulness of the arrest was only affected when the police had failed to give the reason for arrest when it was practicable to do so. In *Murray v. Ministry of Defence* [1988] 1 W.L.R. 692 the House of Lords held that delay by soldiers in Northern Ireland in informing a woman of the fact of her arrest was acceptable. The European Court of Human Rights subsequently found no breach of the Convention.

KEY PRINCIPLE: *Police and Criminal Evidence Act, s. 24:*

"(6) Where a constable has reasonable grounds for suspecting that an arrestable offence has been committed, he may arrest without a warrant anyone whom he has reasonable grounds for suspecting to be guilty of the offence."

Hussien v. Chong Fook Kam

Malaysian police were entitled under the Criminal Procedure Code to arrest on reasonable suspicion of an offence having been committed. A piece of wood fell off a passing lorry and killed a passenger in a car. The police traced the lorry and arrested two men and detained them overnight. The following day they were released because there was insufficient evidence. Their action for damages for false imprisonment was dismissed by the High Court, but allowed on appeal by the Federal Court on the basis that what the police knew at the time was insufficient to establish a prima facie case. The prosecutor appealed.

HELD: (PC) Although the police had good reason to suspect that the one of the arrested men was the driver of the lorry from which the wood fell, that was a long way from suspecting the driver of reckless or dangerous driving. They might not have been aware at the time that the wood had fallen from the lorry, and it might not have occurred to them that it would have caused death. The test used by the Federal Court was wrong. Suspicion could take into account matters that could not be put in evidence in court and need amount to no more than reasonable suspicion. [1970] A.C. 942

Holgate-Mohammed v. Duke

A woman was arrested on suspicion of theft. The police officer questioned her at the station but she was not charged and was released after six hours. She brought an action against the chief constable for wrongful arrest. The judge found the constable had had reasonable suspicion and the period of detention was not excessive. But the constable had wrongfully exercised the power of arrest by deciding not to interview her under caution but to subject her to arrest and detention in the hope of obtaining a confession. The judge's decision was overturned on appeal and the plaintiff appealed.

HELD: (HL) An arrestable offence had been committed and the constable had reasonable grounds to suspect the plaintiff. He was entitled to arrest her for interrogation. The fact that she might confess more readily if arrested and questioned at the police station was a relevant consideration which the constable was entitled to take into account, so the arrest was not unlawful. [1984] A.C. 437

COMMENTARY
In this case the House of Lords confirmed that the police in exercising their statutory powers must satisfy the relevant statutory conditions and must also act within *Wednesbury* principles (see page 81). In exercising their discretion they must not act in a way that was so unreasonable that no reasonable officer could have exercised it in that way. Furthermore, officers must not take irrelevant considerations into account or fail to take into account relevant ones.

KEY PRINCIPLE: *Reasonable suspicion requires answering "yes" to the following questions: "Did the arresting officer suspect the person to be guilty?" (a subjective test) and "was there a reasonable cause for suspicion?" (an objective test).*

Castorina v. Chief Constable of Surrey

The plaintiff was a former employee of a company that was burgled. Detectives who had concluded that the burglary was an inside job arrested her, held her for four hours and then freed her without charge. She brought an action for wrongful arrest. The judge awarded her damages on the basis that the police did not have sufficient material to found a reasonable suspicion that she was the burglar. The police appealed.

HELD: (CA) On the facts the arresting officers had reasonable cause to suspect the plaintiff. The appeal would be allowed. [1988] N.L.J. 180

COMMENTARY
Reasonable suspicion is not defined in PACE and here again the court seemed to be giving guidance that only a fairly low level of suspicion was required.

KEY PRINCIPLE: *There is no common law power to detain for questioning without arrest.*

Rice v. Connolly

The defendant was seen by a police officer in an area where there had been several break-ins. He refused to give his name and address, nor would he accompany the officer to a police box unless arrested. He was convicted of obstructing the officer in the execution of his duty. He appealed.

HELD: (DC) Every citizen had a moral or social duty to assist the police, but there was no such legal duty and the defendant in refusing to answer the police officer's questions was within his common law rights. He had not "wilfully" obstructed the policeman, even though his attitude made it more difficult for the officer to carry out his duty. [1966] 2 Q.B. 414

COMMENTARY
This pre-PACE case gives guidance on the borderline between legitimate and illegitimate disobedience to police orders or requests. Three tests must be satisfied if liability for and offence under what is now section 89 of the Police Act 1996 is to be made out. The officer must be acting in the execution of his duty; secondly, the defendant must do an act which made it more difficult for the officer to carry out that duty; and thirdly' the defendant must have acted wilfully. The case must now be set in the context of the abrogation of the "right to silence" in CJPOA 1994 (see page 110). It must be stressed that the citizen who does not co-operate in police questioning under certain conditions incurs only possible evidential consequences not civil or criminal liability for failure to respond.

KEY PRINCIPLE: *Refusal to answer police questions accompanied by abusive language may give grounds for arrest for obstruction.*

Ricketts v. Cox

Police officers looking for youths responsible for a serious assault approached the defendant early one morning and questioned him. He was unco-operative, abusive and hostile and tried to walk away from the officers. He was convicted of obstructing the police in the execution of their duty and appealed.

HELD: (DC) On the facts there was no doubt that he had committed the offence. (1981) 74 Cr.App.R. 298.

COMMENTARY
The feature that was present in *Ricketts v. Cox* but not in *Rice v. Connelly* was abusive language and behaviour by the

defendant. This arguably is the lowest level of behaviour which could qualify as obstructive.

KEY PRINCIPLE: *The police may be acting in the course of their duty in using minimal restraint in detaining to ask questions without an arrest.*

Donnelly v. Jackman

The defendant was approached by a police officer in the street who wanted to ask him about a recent offence. The defendant ignored the officer's request to stop. The officer touched the defendant on the shoulder intending to stop him to speak to him, but not to charge or arrest him, and the defendant struck the officer. He was convicted of assaulting a constable in the execution of his duty. He appealed.

HELD: (DC) The police officer was not acting outside the ambit of his duties in trying to stop the defendant in order to speak to him. The conviction would stand. Not every trivial interference with a citizen's liberty amounted to a course of conduct sufficient to take an officer out of the course of his duties. [1970] 1 W.L.R. 562

Collins v. Wilcock

The defendant and another woman, a known prostitute, were seen apparently soliciting men in the street. The defendant refused to be questioned by police and tried to walk away. When an officer tried to restrain her she scratched his arm and was arrested and charged with assaulting an officer in the execution of her duty. She was convicted and appealed.

HELD: (DC) It was unlawful for a police officer to use force to try to stop and detain another person without using the power of arrest. Police could caution suspects under the Street Offences Act 1959 but had no power to stop and detain a woman to implement the system of cautioning. The police officer had not been acting in the course of her duty when she tried to restrain the defendant, and the conviction would be quashed. [1984] 1 W.L.R. 1172

COMMENTARY

These two cases illustrate the scope of the test to be applied to establish if the officer is acting in the execution of his duty in making physical contact with a citizen. In *Collins* there had been an unjustified detention by the police officer since the relevant statute, the Street Offences Act 1959, did not authorise detention. The test set out in that case was whether taking into account the nature of his duty his use of physical contact in the face of non-co-operation persisted beyond generally acceptable standards of conduct. In *Donnelly*, which was referred to in *Wilcock*, Talbot J. had said not every trivial interference with a citizen's liberty amounted to a course of conduct sufficient to take the officer out of the course of his duties.

Breach of the Peace

KEY PRINCIPLE: *At common law power to arrest is available to a constable and a private citizen where either a breach of the peace is committed in the presence of the person making the arrest; or where the arrestor reasonably believes that such a breach will be committed in the immediate future by the person arrested although he has not yet committed any breach; or where a breach of the peace has been committed and it is reasonably believed that a renewal of it is threatened.*

R. v. Howell

Police were called to a disturbance in the street during the early hours outside a house where a party was taking place. They asked a group including the defendant to move on. The defendant among others swore at the police and was told he would be arrested for disturbing the police if he continued. The defendant argued with the policeman and a fight developed. He was charged with resisting arrest. At trial the defendant submitted that there was no case to answer because the prosecution had failed to show that any violence had been used before the arrest and because the defendant had merely used reasonable force to resist unlawful arrest. The defendant was convicted and appealed.

HELD: (CA) A constable or a private citizen could arrest without warrant if he reasonably and honestly believed that a breach of the peace was about to be committed. Where an arrest was made for an anticipated breach of the peace it was enough for a valid arrest for the constable to say the arrest was for "breach of the peace". Threat of violence was sufficient to constitute a breach of the peace. [1982] Q.B. 416

COMMENTARY

The ingredients of a breach of the peace may also give rise to arrest powers under PACE but the private citizen under PACE cannot lawfully arrest on the basis of reasonable belief that an offence may occur. In addition the public order offences under POA and CJPOA give specific powers of arrest to constables and the elements of the statutory offences will overlap with the factors involved in breach of the peace. (See Chapter 11).

Albert v. Lavin

The defendant jumped a bus queue, several of whom objected. A plain clothes police constable tried to prevent the defendant getting on the bus. There was a struggle and the constable pulled him away from the queue. The constable said he was a police officer but the defendant did not believe him and struck him several times. The constable arrested him for assaulting a constable in the execution of his duty. The magistrates held that the defendant's reaction to being prevented from boarding the bus was a continuing breach of the peace. Though he genuinely believed the constable was not a police officer he had no reasonable grounds for that belief. If he had been unlawfully detained he had used only reasonable force to effect his release. The man appealed.

HELD: (HL) Every citizen had a right to prevent a breach or threatened breach of the peace. Reasonable steps to do so could include detaining the peace-breaker against his will. The defendant's assault on the constable would not have been justified even had the constable not been a policeman, so it was irrelevant whether he had acted in the belief that he was not. [1982] A.C. 546

KEY PRINCIPLE: *The police may arrest for obstruction those who ignore their request for action aimed at avoiding a threat of immediate and imminent violence.*

Moss v. McLachlan

Striking miners on their way to picket in Nottinghamshire were stopped at a road block where police told them to turn back on the grounds that they feared a breach of the peace. The miners tried to push through the police cordon and were arrested for obstructing the police in the execution of their duty. They were convicted and appealed by way of case stated.

HELD: (DC) The police honestly and on reasonable grounds feared a breach of the peace if the miners were allowed to proceed. They were therefore acting in the execution of their duty in stopping the pickets. A constable who apprehends a breach of the peace is under a duty to prevent it. It could not be held that the police could only stop the men if it was clear from their words and deeds that they intended a breach of the peace. The defendants had been rightly convicted. [1985] I.R.L.R.76

COMMENTARY
The case illustrates the important connection between the lawfulness of an arrest and the requirements of obstructing the police in the execution of their duty now section 89 of the Police Act 1996.

KEY PRINCIPLE: *Section 34, Criminal Justice and Public Order Act 1994:*

"(1) Where, in any proceedings against a person for an offence, evidence is given that the accused—(a) at any time before he was charged with the offence, on being questioned under caution by a constable trying to discover whether or by whom the offence had been committed, failed to mention any fact relied on in his defence in those proceedings . . . (d) the court or jury, in determining whether the accused is guilty of the offence charged, may draw such inferences from the failure as appear proper."

KEY PRINCIPLE: *Legal advice not to answer questions at police interview will not in itself amount to sufficient reason for not mentioning relevant matters which may be later relied on by the defendant.*

R. v. Condron
Heroin addicts were arrested on drug charges. Their solicitor considered them unfit to answer questions because of their withdrawal symptoms, and advised them to say nothing at interview. The police doctor considered them fit. They gave no answers at interview. At trial, it was submitted the jury should be told not to draw adverse inferences from the interview evidence because they had refused to answer on legal advice. The judge directed that it was a matter for the jury whether or not to draw adverse inferences.

HELD: (CA) A properly directed jury could draw adverse inferences if they concluded that the failure to answer could only be attributed to the defendant's guilt. [1997] 1 W.L.R. 827

COMMENTARY

Legal advisors have difficult options to weigh up faced with defendants who may be emotionally or physically vulnerable and thus arguably not in a position to be interviewed. If the suspect follows advice to remain silent, adverse inferences may be drawn at trial. See also *R. v. Cowan* [1996] Q.B. 373

Questioning-Detention-Confessions

KEY PRINCIPLE: *Police and Criminal Evidence Act 1984, s. 76:*

> "(2) If, in any proceedings where the prosecution proposes to give in evidence a confession made by an accused person, it is represented to the court that the confession was or may have been obtained—(a) by oppression of the person who made it; or (b) in consequence of anything said or done which was likely, in the circumstances existing at the time, to render unreliable any confession which might be made by him in consequence thereof, the court shall not allow the confession to be given in evidence against him except in so far as the prosecution proves to the court beyond reasonable doubt that the confession (notwithstanding that it may be true) was not obtained as aforesaid."

KEY PRINCIPLE: *Oppression is to be given its dictionary meaning.*

R. v. Fulling

The prosecution at the defendant's trial sought to adduce a confession she had made after persistent questioning. She wanted the judge to exclude the confession under section 76 of PACE on the basis that the prosecution had not proved it was not obtained by oppression. The judge ruled that oppression meant something over and above the oppression normal to police custody and dismissed her application. She appealed.

HELD: (CA) The word "oppression" was to be given its ordinary dictionary meaning of "the exercise of authority in a burdensome harsh or wrongful manner; unjust or cruel treatment of subjects". It was thought that most invariably this would involve some impropriety by the interrogator. [1987] 1 Q.B. 426

COMMENTARY

This case amplifies the non-exhaustive definition of oppression contained in section 76(8): "In this section oppression includes torture, inhuman or degrading treatment and the use or threat of violence (whether or not amounting to torture)". The test as set out in *Fulling* on its face could mean that any breach of the Act or Codes could amount to oppression. However, this wider interpretation has been precluded by the courts since it is stressed in *Fulling* impropriety on the part of the police was required before the section could apply. In *Hughes* (see below) it became clear that the terms "wrongful and improper" required an element of deliberate abuse of power or bad faith. Furthermore, in practice the courts have reserved this section for the most serious acts of misconduct by the police, thus although bad faith is a necessary precondition it is not a sufficient one. The exercise of discretion under PACE, section 78 is more usually applied to deliberate misuse of police power. The stress on the state of mind of the alleged oppressor rather than the effect on the detainee has been the subject of academic criticism.

KEY PRINCIPLE: *The test under PACE, section 76(2)(b) requires both "something said or done" and "circumstances existing at the time" to have a causal effect on making any confession so obtained unreliable.*

R. v. Harvey

The defendant, who was a psychopathic alcoholic of low intelligence, was charged with murder. With her lesbian lover, she had been present when the murder occurred. Both women were arrested close to the scene of the crime. On arrest, in the presence of the defendant, the other woman confessed to the crime. The following day the defendant confessed. The other woman retracted her confession, became a Crown witness, but died before the trial. At trial the only evidence against her was the confession. The defence sought to have the confession excluded.

HELD: (CCC) The judge was not satisfied beyond reasonable doubt that the confession was not obtained as a result of the defendant's having heard her lover's confession. The defendant's confession would be excluded and the jury instructed to acquit. [1988] Crim. L.R. 241

COMMENTARY

The application of the "two limbs of the reliability" test is set out in this case. There are two aspects, namely "something said or done"; (here hearing the first confession of the lover "in the 'circumstances existing at the time' (here the mental state of the defendant"). In practice the section is frequently reserved for the vulnerable defendant, *i.e.* one whose mental or emotional state makes what is said or done likely to affect the reliability of any confession made under those circumstances. Another feature of the test is that there is no need for police impropriety.

R. v. Goldenberg

A heroin addict requested an interview five days after his arrest on a charge of conspiracy to supply drugs. At the interview he gave information about his heroin supplier. His counsel argued at trial that the interview might be unreliable because the admissions were made to get bail and he might be expected to say anything to feed his addiction.

HELD: (CA) The words "said or done" in section 76(2)(b) do not include anything said or done by the person making the confession. (1988) 88 Cr.App.R. 285

COMMENTARY

Here in a controversial decision the Court held that the "something said or done" cannot be something self-inflicted by the defendant.

KEY PRINCIPLE: *Police and Criminal Evidence Act 1984, s. 78:*

"(1) In any proceedings the court may refuse to allow evidence on which the prosecution proposes to rely to be given if it appears to the court that, having regard to all the circumstances, including the circumstances in which the evidence was obtained, the admission of the evidence would have such an adverse effect on the fairness of the proceedings that the court ought not to admit it. (2) Nothing in this section shall prejudice any rule of law requiring a court to exclude evidence."

KEY PRINCIPLE: *A breach or breaches of PACE particularly section 58 or the Code in the absence of bad faith on the part of the police may lead to exclusion of confession evidence if it has caused the defendant to confess.*

R. v. Samuel

The defendant was arrested for armed robbery. His request to see a solicitor was refused under section 58 of PACE. He was questioned and confessed to two burglaries but denied robbery. He was charged with the burglaries but his solicitor was denied access. The defendant was again questioned and eventually confessed to the robbery, whereupon he was charged and allowed to see his solicitor. He appealed on the grounds that the judge should have ruled the final interview inadmissible.

HELD: (CA) The denial of access by the police could not be properly continued once the defendant had been charged so that there was no power to prevent the defendant consulting a solicitor after he had been charged. In any event the police had to show that there were reasonable grounds to believe that the solicitor would deliberately or accidentally warn other suspects or hamper the recovery of property. There were no grounds for thinking that the respected and experienced solicitor involved would do so. The conviction would be quashed. [1988] 1 Q.B. 615

COMMENTARY
In this case the Court of Appeal held that in failing to allow access to a solicitor "the appellant was denied improperly one of the most important and fundamental rights of the citizen". Here it was significant that the appellant was not a persistent criminal and was thus less likely to be able to handle the interview without legal advice. Section 58 allows delay in access to a solicitor if certain conditions are met. Here they are not.

KEY PRINCIPLE: *The presence or absence of bad faith on the part of the police will affect the exercise of the court's discretion to exclude confession evidence obtained by a breach of PACE or the Codes.*

R. v. Alladice

The defendant was interviewed by police after an armed robbery and according to them admitted involvement. He was asked if he wanted a solicitor and said he did though he refused to sign to that effect. He was convicted and appealed on the basis that his admissions ought to have been excluded because he had been denied access to a solicitor.

HELD: (CA) Though section 58 had been breached, there was no suggestion of oppression and no reason to believe the absence of a solicitor rendered the confession unreliable. The judge had rejected the allegation that the police had invented his confession. The conviction would be upheld. (1988) 87 Cr.App.R. 380

COMMENTARY

The factor which distinguished this case from *Samuel* was that the appellant was criminally experienced who knew his rights regardless of the presence of a solicitor. In addition the court considered that the absence of bad faith on the part of the police was significant thus suggesting *obiter* that a deliberate breach of section 58 will certainly lead to exclusion under section 78.

R. v. Mason

The defendant was arrested for setting fire to a motor car. During questioning police officers untruthfully told him his fingerprints had been found on glass fragments in the car. They told the same lie to his solicitor. The solicitor advised him to explain any involvement he had in the incident, and the defendant confessed that he had got a friend to do it. The judge held the confession admissible and the defendant appealed.

HELD: (CA) The confession ought to have been excluded. The judge had failed to take account of the deception practised on the defendant's solicitor, whose duty it was to advise the defendant unfettered by false information from the police. [1988] 1 W.L.R. 139

COMMENTARY

Another illustration that deliberate misuse of police power in investigating an offence will render a confession inadmissible.

R. v. Hughes

The defendant was convicted of deception and handling on the basis of admissions made at interview. He had been arrested on a Saturday afternoon in winter and taken to a police station more than 100 miles away where he was put into a cold cell. He asked for a duty solicitor but was wrongly told none was available. He said he would be interviewed without a solicitor. In the course of the interview he made damaging admissions. He appealed on the basis that his admissions should have been excluded under section 78(1) of PACE.

HELD: (CA) Section 78 required consideration first of the circumstances in which the interview came to the conducted, then the question whether its admission would have an adverse effect on the fairness of the trial. The judge was satisfied that the appellant genuinely consented to be interviewed, even though he was not aware of the true state of affairs, because he was cold and unhappy. The judge had to balance the interests of the prosecution and those of the defence in deciding where justice lay. [1988] Crim. L.R. 519

COMMENTARY

Here the Court of Appeal also considered the operation of the oppression test and considered that denial of legal advice due to a misunderstanding not bad faith on the part of the police could not lead to exclusion under this section. Here as in *Mason* the cases do not make it clear when section 78 and when section 76(2) (b) is appropriate for deliberate malpractice.

KEY PRINCIPLE: *Serious and substantial breaches of PACE and Code C should lead to exclusion of evidence obtained thereby.*

R. v. Canale

The defendant was interviewed by police in connection with a series of robberies. At two interviews he allegedly admitted providing the robbers with a shotgun and driving the getaway vehicle. Contrary to the PACE Code of Practice, these interviews were not contemporaneously recorded, nor was any reason recorded for failing to do so. Two subsequent interviews were recorded contemporaneously and at them the defendant made similar admissions. At trial, the defendant sought to exclude the interviews but the judge admitted them. The defendant then gave evidence that the admissions at interview had been made as a result of a trick. He was convicted and appealed on the basis that the conviction was unsafe and unsatisfactory.

HELD: (CA) Because of the absence of a contemporary record of the first two interviews, the judge had been deprived of the very evidence he needed to enable him to decide whether the interviews were admissible. The jury, too, had been deprived of evidence which would have enabled them to decide the truth of the defendant's story. The police officers had flagrantly and deliberately breached the code and the judge should have used his discretion to keep out the interviews. [1990] 2 All E.R. 187

COMMENTARY

This case is an interesting example of the difference between sections 76(2)(b) and 78. The former was considered not to be appropriate since as the appellant had been in the Parachute Regiment he was not in the same position as a vulnerable defendant faced with police questions.

Exclusion of Non-confession Evidence

KEY PRINCIPLE: *There is no discretion for a court to exclude evidence that is relevant solely on the grounds that there has been some impropriety in the way it has been obtained.*

Jeffrey v. Black

Two drugs squad officers arrested the defendant for stealing a sandwich in a pub. He was charged and the officers searched his lodgings where they found cannabis. At his trial for possession of cannabis the justices found the defendant had not consented to his room being searched and ruled the evidence inadmissible because the police had had no authority. The prosecutor appealed.

Held: (CA) The police officers should either have obtained the defendant's consent or a search warrant. As it was their entry and search was unlawful and the drug evidence had been irregularly obtained. However, the test whether evidence was admissible was whether it was relevant and not whether it had been properly obtained. The drug evidence was relevant and the magistrates were wrong to exclude it. [1978] Q.B. 490

KEY PRINCIPLE: *There is no common law discretion to exclude evidence solely on the grounds that it has been obtained by entrapment.*

R. v. Sang

Two defendants were charged with conspiring to pass forged banknotes. At trial their counsel sought to establish that the facts alleged against them came about through the activities of an agent provocateur. The judge ruled that he had no discretion to exclude evidence for that reason. The defendants then changed their plea and were sentenced. The court of appeal upheld the judge's ruling. One of the defendants appealed.

HELD: (HL) The judge always had a discretion to exclude evidence if its prejudicial effect outweighed its probative value. But apart from admissions and confessions and evidence obtained from the accused after commission of the offence, there was no discretion to exclude evidence even if it had been obtained improperly or unfairly. The fact that the evidence was the result of an agent provocateur's activities was no reason to exclude it. [1980] A.C. 402

COMMENTARY

This case confirmed that entrapment was not a defence and that if the discretion was used to exclude evidence this would amount to a procedural device to circumvent a matter of substantive law. In addition the House was whittling down the discretion to exclude evidence at all under the common law to cases where the prejudicial effect would outweigh the probative value. The following cases however indicate however a more robust stand on the part of the courts to exclude evidence to protect rights.

KEY PRINCIPLE: *Impropriety in the obtaining of evidence, including entrapment, may be a factor leading to the exclusion of evidence under section 78 of PACE.*

R. v. Christou; R. v. Wright

Undercover police officers set up a bogus jewellery shop which bought stolen goods. The aim was to recover stolen goods and obtain evidence against those who had either stolen or dishonestly handled the goods. The defendants were among those who sold stolen goods to the shop. At their trial, the judge refused a defence submission that the evidence ought to be excluded either because it had been obtained by a trick or because in the course of their bogus dealings the police had questioned the men without first having cautioned them contrary to Code C of the Codes of Practice. The judge concluded that admission of the evidence would not affect the fairness of the trial under section 78 of the Police and Criminal Evidence Act 1984. The defendants appealed.

HELD: (CA) The judge had properly exercised his discretion. Code C was intended to protect suspects who were vulnerable to abuse or pressure from police officers and applied where a suspect was being questioned by an officer acting as such for the purpose of obtaining evidence. Here there was no question of pressure or intimidation and the parties were on equal terms. It would be wrong for police officers to adopt an undercover pose or disguise in order to circumvent the requirements of Code C. [1992] 1 Q.B. 979

R. v. Smurthwaite

In two separate cases a man had made arrangements with what he thought was a contract killer to have his wife murdered. In both cases the supposed contract killers were undercover police officers who tape-recorded their meetings. Both were convicted and contended on appeal that any prosecution evidence which came from an agent provocateur or was obtained by a trick should be excluded under section 78 of the Police and Criminal Evidence Act 1984.

HELD: (CA) The judge had no discretion to exclude otherwise admissible evidence merely because it had been obtained improperly or unfairly. It remained a substantive rule of law that entrapment or the use of an agent provocateur was not of itself a defence to a criminal charge. The tape recordings were an accurate and unchallenged record of the offences being committed and had properly been admitted in evidence. [1994] 1 All E.R. 898

COMMENTARY
These cases confirm that section 78 had not altered the substantive rule of law whereby entrapment or use of an agent

provocateur is not a defence to a criminal charge. However, entrapment is not irrelevant to a consideration of whether to use the discretion to exclude under section 78. The court must consider whether in all the circumstances the obtaining of the evidence in that way would have an adverse effect on the fairness of the proceedings. This involves considering fairness to the public as well as fairness to the accused.

R. v. Khan (Sultan)

The defendant was convicted of involvement in importing heroin. The evidence against him came from an electronic listening device installed by the police in a private house visited by the defendant. He appealed against conviction on the basis that the evidence should have been excluded under section 78 of the Police and Criminal Evidence Act 1984.

HELD: (HL) There was no right of privacy in English law. Relevant evidence remained admissible, despite being obtained improperly or unlawfully, subject to the court's discretion to exclude it. Although an apparent breach of Article 8 of the European Convention on Human Rights could be relevant in considering whether to exclude evidence, it was not determinative per se, as an appellant's rights were safeguarded under section 78 which provided for a review of the admissibility of evidence. [1996] 3 W.L.R. 162

Powers of Entry Search and Seizure

KEY PRINCIPLE: *Under the common law the police may seize articles which may be evidence of grave offences irrespective of whether the officer is lawfully on the premises at the time.*

Chic Fashions (West Wales) Ltd v. Jones

The plaintiff's premises were searched by police looking for stolen goods. The warrant authorised a search for goods stolen from a particular manufacturer. The search revealed no goods from that manufacturer, but the police seized other goods which they believed might have been stolen. They eventually accepted the plaintiff's explanation and returned the goods. The plaintiff sued the chief constable for damages for trespass. The county court judge gave judgment for the plaintiff and the chief constable appealed.

HELD: (CA) Where a constable entered a house on a search warrant for stolen goods he could seize any goods which he reasonably believed to be stolen, whether or not they were specified in the warrant. The appeal would be allowed. [1968] 2 Q.B. 299

Ghani v. Jones

Police inquiring into a woman's disappearance searched her father-in-law's house without a warrant and took away his passport and those of his wife and daughter. The passport-holders, who were Pakistanis, brought an action for the return of their passports to allow them to visit Pakistan. The police maintained that the passports might be evidence if and when they arrested those responsible for the woman's disappearance. They were ordered to return the passports and appealed.

HELD: (CA) The police had power to seize evidence of grave offences, under the common law, and it did not depend on the officer being lawfully on the premises. The police had not shown reasonable grounds for believing that the documents were material evidence, and would be ordered to return them forthwith. [1970] 1 Q.B. 693

COMMENTARY
The law relating to searches and seizure is now largely contained in PACE but section 19(5) of PACE states "The powers conferred by this section are in addition to any power otherwise conferred". If this incudes common law powers then cases such as these cover the law relating to trespassing constables.

---

11. FREEDOM OF ASSEMBLY

Public Meetings

1. Public Meetings in Private Places

KEY PRINCIPLE: *The police may enter and remain on private premises if they have reasonable grounds for believing that if they were not present a breach of the peace might occur.*

Thomas v. Sawkins

Some 600 people attended a meeting in the Caerau library to protest against the Incitement to Disaffection Act. Police officers were refused admission but insisted on entering it and remaining there during the meeting. One of the convenors of the meeting brought an information against a police sergeant that he had unlawfully assaulted him.

HELD: (DC) The officers were entitled in the execution of their duty to prevent the commission of any offence or breach of the peace, to enter and remain on the premises. [1935] 2 K.B. 249

COMMENTARY
This is a controversial decision. Commentators have argued that its scope should be limited to those situations where a meeting has been advertised as public and the police have reasonable grounds for believing that a breach of the peace will occur if the police are not present. That is to say it would not allow police to enter private premises to attend a meeting which is not advertised as open to the public. Furthermore, although the court's decision appears to allow entry by the police before the offence is imminent compare this formulation with that in *R. v. Howell* (see page 108) where the Court of Appeal held that the power of the police only arises if a breach of the peace is imminent.

Public Meetings in Public Places

KEY PRINCIPLE: *On the highway any one has the prima facie right to pass or repass along it and to make any necessary stops such as for rest. But people have no right to stop on the highway unreasonably.*

Harrison v. Duke of Rutland

The defendant was the owner of a grouse moor crossed by a highway, though the soil belonged to him. The plaintiff went on the highway during a shoot, with the aim of interfering with the shooting by preventing the grouse from going towards the guns. The duke's keepers forced him off the highway and he brought an action for assault. The duke counter-claimed for a declaration that he was a trespasser.

HELD: (CA) Granting the declaration sought by the duke, that the plaintiff was a trespasser in so far as he was on the

highway for a purpose other than its use as a highway. [1893] 1
Q.B. 142

R. v. Clarke (No. 2)

The field secretary of the Campaign for Nuclear Disarmament
led a crowd through the streets during a demonstration against
the Greek royal couple. He was convicted of inciting persons to
commit a public nuisance by obstructing the highway and
sentenced to 18 months imprisonment. He appealed.

HELD: (DC) The judge had failed to direct the jury on the
question whether granted obstruction there was unreasonable
use of the highway. He had told the jury that if there was
physical obstruction then the defendant was guilty. The appeal
was allowed. [1964] 2 Q.B. 315

COMMENTARY

This case illustrates the application of the common law
offence of public nuisance in blocking the highway. It illustrates that the disruption involved must amount to unreasonable use of the highway for liability to be incurred. A similar
interpretation has been applied to the application of the Highways Act (see *Nagy v. Weston* page 124).

KEY PRINCIPLE: *Highways Act s. 137:*

> "(1) If a person, without lawful authority or excuse, in any way
> wilfully obstructs the free passage along a highway he shall
> be guilty of an offence . . ."

KEY PRINCIPLE: Mens rea *in this offence does not require
knowingly doing a wrongful act.*

Arrowsmith v. Jenkins

The defendant addressed a public meeting in the street in
Bootle and attracted a crowd which blocked the road for five
minutes, until police with her assistance cleared a path for
vehicles. She was accused of wilfully obstructing the highway
and was convicted by justices. She appealed on the grounds
that the prosecution had failed to establish a knowingly wrongful act on her part.

HELD: (DC) A person who without lawful authority or excuse did an act which caused obstruction was guilty of an offence. *Mens rea* in the sense that a person would only be guilty if she knowingly did a wrongful act could not be inferred from the words "wilfully obstructs". [1963] 2 Q.B. 561

COMMENTARY
This decision gives a great deal of licence to the police. It is arguable that the defendant intended to cause an obstruction but describing such conduct as wilful has incurred much criticism.

KEY PRINCIPLE: *To commit an offence the user of the highway must act unreasonably.*

Nagy v. Weston
A hot-dog seller parked in a lay-by near a bus stop for five minutes and refused to move on when asked by a police officer to do so. He was convicted of wilfully obstructing the highway and appealed on the ground that for an obstruction to be wilful it must lack lawful authority or reasonable excuse.

HELD: (DC) Appeal dismissed. Excuse and reasonableness were really the same. It was a question of fact in each case whether the defendant had used the highway unreasonably. [1965] 1 W.L.R. 280

Hirst and Agu v. Chief Constable of West Yorkshire
Members of an animal rights group who protested outside a fur shop were convicted by justices of obstructing the highway. On appeal to the Crown Court, it was held that their actions were not incidental to lawful use of the highway so the conviction should stand. They appealed by case stated.

HELD: (DC) Justices should consider whether there was an obstruction, whether it was deliberate and then whether it was without lawful authority or excuse. This embraced activities otherwise lawful in themselves which might or might not be reasonable in all the circumstances mentioned in *Nagy v. Weston*. The courts recognised a right to demonstrate and should allow freedom to protest on issues of public concern. (1986) 85 Cr.App.R. 143

COMMENTARY
These two cases mark some liberalisation from the decision in *Arrowsmith*. The stress on the purpose of the obstruction and the reminder in *Hirst* and *Agu* that the courts should have regard to the freedom to demonstrate suggest that using an assembly as a means of protest may amount to a reasonable use of the highway.

KEY PRINCIPLE: *A breach of the peace will arise if an act is done or threatened to be done which either harms a person or in his presence his property or is likely to cause such harm or which puts a person in fear of such harm.*

Piddington v. Bates

In the course of a strike, the front and back entrances of a printworks were picketed. A police officer declared that only two pickets were needed at the back door, whereupon the defendant tried to pass to go to the back entrance to join the two pickets there and was arrested. The defendant was convicted of obstructing the police officer and appealed.

HELD: (DC) The mere statement by a constable that he anticipated a breach of the peace was not enough to justify his taking action to prevent it. But that on the facts there was a real danger of a breach of the peace and the defendant had been rightly convicted. [1961] 1 W.L.R. 162

COMMENTARY
The vagueness of the definition of breach of the peace (see *Howell*, page 108) means that is at times employed to deal with a public order problem on occasions where the statutory powers might not be suitable. Here, in effect, the courts sanctioned the police placing a limit on the number of pickets when there was no statutory maximum number. (See also *Moss v. MacLachan*, page 109).

KEY PRINCIPLE: *Trade Union and Labour Relations (Consolidation) Act 1992, s. 220:*

"(1) It is lawful for a person in contemplation or furtherance of a trade dispute to attend—(a) at or near his own place of work, or (b) if he is an official of a trade union, at or near the place of work of a member of the union whom he is accompanying and whom he represents, for the purpose only of peacefully obtaining or communicating information, or peacefully persuading any person to work or abstain from working."

KEY PRINCIPLE: *Injunctions may be granted if pickets carry out for which there is no statutory immunity.*

Thomas v. National Union of Mineworkers (South Wales Area)

South Wales miners joined the national strike on March 12, 1984, but in November a few returned to work. The collieries where they worked were picketed by 50 to 70 strikers, who threatened them as they were driven across the picket line. They sought injunctions restraining unlawful picketing.

HELD: The attendance of some 50 to 70 strikers each day shouting abuse at the plaintiffs could not be picketing for the purpose of peacefully persuading them not to work. The working miners were entitled to enjoy their right to use the highway without unreasonable harassment. [1986] Ch. 20

COMMENTARY

Here although no obvious civil offence such as assault was being perpetrated the court was in effect extending the definition of an existing tort. Mass picketing was "unreasonable interference with the plaintiff's right to use the highway".

KEY PRINCIPLE: *There is a general presumption in favour of protecting the exercise of free lawful expression in public and private.*

Hubbard v. Pitt

Campaigners opposed to the gentrification of part of north London picketed local estate agents, who sued for nuisance and libel and obtained an injunction restraining the picketing. The plaintiffs appealed.

HELD: (CA) Dismissing the appeal (Lord Denning dissenting) that the injunction should continue until trial. The injunction was not too wide, and there was a serious issue to be tried. (*Per* Lord Denning M.R.) the rights to demonstrate and protest are rights which it is in the public interest that individuals should possess and exercise. [1976] 1 Q.B. 142

COMMENTARY
Lord Denning's comments are of ten cited as illustrating the close relationship of freedoms of speech and assembly.

KEY PRINCIPLE: *Public Order Act 1986, s. 4:*

"(1) A person is guilty of an offence if he—(a) uses towards another person threatening, abusive or insulting words or behaviour, or (b) distributes or displays to another person any writing, sign or other visible representation which is threatening, abusive or insulting, with intent to cause that person to believe that immediate unlawful violence will be used against him or another by any person, or to provoke the immediate use of unlawful violence by that person or another, or whereby that person is likely to believe that such violence will be used or it is likely that such violence will be provoked."

KEY PRINCIPLE: *The meaning of the word insulting is a matter of fact, not law, and it should be given its natural meaning.*

Brutus v. Cozens
The defendant disrupted play at Wimbledon when a South African was playing. As a protest against apartheid, he and others distributed leaflets to the crowd while preventing play. They were acquitted of insulting behaviour because the justices held that their behaviour had not been insulting. The prosecutor appealed to the Divisional Court, which held that the justices' findings established insulting behaviour. The defendant appealed.

HELD: (HL) The meaning of "insulting" was not a question of law. It was an ordinary English word. It was not unreasonable for the tribunal to conclude that the defendant's behaviour had not been insulting. The defendant's behaviour was deplorable but it did not insult the spectators. [1973] A.C. 854

COMMENTARY

In disagreeing with the Divisional Court's interpretation of the word insulting, namely that which affronted others, the House of Lords observed that Parliament had to solve the difficult question of how far freedom of speech or behaviour must be limited in the general public interest. It considered (*per* Lord Reid) that "it would have been going much too far to prohibit all speech or conduct likely to occasion a breach of the peace because determined opponents may not shrink from organising or at least threatening a breach of the peace in order to silence a speaker whose views they detest."

KEY PRINCIPLE: *Such violence means immediate unlawful violence.*

R. v. Horseferry Road Metropolitan Magistrat, ex p. Siadatan

The applicant laid an information against Penguin Books, the publishers of "The Satanic Verses", claiming that it contained abusive and insulting writing whereby unlawful violence would be provoked. The magistrates refused a summons on the grounds that the applicant had failed to demonstrate a likelihood of immediate violence. The applicant sought judicial review.

HELD: (DC) Dismissing the application, that of two possible readings of a penal statute the courts should adopt the alternative that limited the scope of the offence created, and the magistrate had correctly refused to issue the summons.

COMMENTARY

This case confirms that section 4 is to be applied primarily in a public order context in stressing the requirement of immediacy so that the insulting language has to be used as part of a public demonstration.

KEY PRINCIPLE *Public Order Act 1986, s. 5:*

"(1) A person is guilty of an offence if he—(a) uses threatening, abusive or insulting words or behaviour, or disorderly behaviour, or (b) displays any writing, sign or other visible representation which is threatening, abusive or insulting, within the hearing or sight of a person likely to be caused harassment, alarm or distress thereby. . . . (3) It is a defence for the accused to prove—. . . (c) that his conduct was reasonable . . ."

KEY PRINCIPLE: *The test of awareness is subjective so to succeed the prosecution must show that the accused is aware of the threatening abusive or insulting nature of the display, etc. The test of reasonableness under section 5(3) (c) is objective.*

DPP v. Clarke, Lewis, O'Connell and O'Keefe

Anti-abortion campaigners were charged with threatening behaviour for showing placards of aborted foetuses outside a clinic. The justices decided that on an objective test the behaviour of the campaigners was not reasonable, but that on the balance of probabilities none of them intended to be threatening, abusive or insulting. They dismissed the informations and the prosecutor appealed.

HELD: (DC) The justices had applied the right tests and the appeal would be dismissed. The defendants were unaware that those seeing the foetus placards would find them threatening. [1992] Crim. L.R. 60

COMMENTARY
Section 5 is one of the most controversial of the new sections of the POA 1986 since it criminalises behaviour which was formerly thought to be too trivial to incur criminal liability, "mere horseplay" in the words of one commentator. This decision makes the prosecution's task more difficult in needing to establish that the defendant was aware his behaviour was likely to cause harassment, etc. However, on the other hand it gives a narrow interpretation to the term reasonable in accepting that it will depend upon what a bench of magistrates considers reasonable.

KEY PRINCIPLE: *A police officer may be a person who is caused harassment alarm or distress under section 5(1).*

Director of Public Prosecutions v. Orum

The defendant was drunk and arguing in the street with his girlfriend in the early hours. Two police officers arrived and one of them told the defendant to be quiet. The defendant told the police officer to go away and threatened to hit him. He was arrested for causing a breach of the peace and kicked and hit the other constable as he was being put into the police car. He was then charged under section 5 of the Public Order Act 1986. The justices found that a police officer could not be a person who could be caused harassment, alarm or distress and dismissed the charge. The prosecutor appealed.

HELD: (DC) It was a question of fact whether a police officer was a person who could be caused harassment, etc. The justices were wrong to find that the officer could not be such a person. [1989] 1 W.L.R. 88

KEY PRINCIPLE: *Public Order Act 1986, s. 14A:*

"(1) If at any time the chief officer of police reasonably believes that an assembly is intended to be held in any district at a place on land to which the public has no right of access or only a limited right of access and that the assembly: (a) is likely to be held without the permission of the occupier of the land or to conduct itself in such a way as to exceed the limits of any permission of his or the limits of the public's right of access; and (b) may result—(i) in serious disruption to the life of the community, or (ii) where the land, or a building or monument on it is of historical architectural, archeological or scientific importance in significant damage to the land, building or monument, he may apply to the council of the district for an order prohibiting for a specified period the holding of all trespassory assemblies in the district or part of it as specified.

KEY PRINCIPLE: *A banning order under this section makes it an offence to assemble on public highways within the exclusion zone.*

Director of Public Prosecutions v. Jones (Margaret)

The defendant was involved in a peaceful demonstration on part of the highway near Stonehenge. The area was subject to an order under section 14 of the Public Order Act 1986 and she and other person were convicted of trespassory assembly. The appealed to the Crown Court, which accepted their argument that a peaceful assembly was not unlawful. The prosecution appealed by way of case stated.

HELD: (DC) Although there was a right of passage over the public highway which also covered anything incidental, an assembly of more than 20 people was not incidental. It exceeded reasonable rights of access allowed by law. Demonstrations were not associated with rights of passage and there was no legal authority allowing a right of assembly on the public highway. [1997] 2 W.L.R. 578

COMMENTARY
In one of the first successful prosecutions under this section, introduced in 1994, the Court confirmed that there was no right in law for a member of the public to hold a peaceful non-obstructive assembly on a public highway.

Preventive Justice

The overriding duty of the police and magistrates to preserve the peace justifies preventive methods to avert disorder even if this means interfering with someone who is not about to commit a breach of the peace or do or join an illegal act but who is likely to be made an object of insult or injury by others who are about to break the peace.

KEY PRINCIPLE: *A group of persons acting lawfully are not to be regarded as acting unlawfully when others make threats to cause a breach of the peace.*

Beatty v. Gilbanks
Members of the Salvation Army marched in procession through Weston-super-Mare, with no intention of breaching the peace, but knowing that they might be opposed by other persons organised in a "Skeleton Army" in a way which would lead to a breach of the peace committed by those others. Salvation Army leaders were arrested and convicted of unlawful assembly. They appealed.

HELD: (DC) The appellants had not been guilty of unlawfully and tumultuously assembling to the disturbance of the peace,

and therefore could not be convicted of unlawful assembly.
(1882) 9 Q.B.D. 559

KEY PRINCIPLE: *The principle expressed in Beatty v.
Gilbanks may be limited if a policemen on the spot had reasonable grounds for believing that dispersing a lawful assembly was the only way of preventing a breach of the peace.*

Duncan v. Jones

A communist activist was about to address a crowd outside a
labour exchange when she was forbidden to do so by a police
officer. She persisted in trying to hold the meeting and
obstructed the officer's attempts to prevent her. Neither she
nor any of the persons present at the meeting committed,
incited or provoked a breach of the peace. The court found
that the officer reasonably apprehended a breach of the peace
would occur if she did address the meeting. She was found
guilty of wilfully obstructing the officer in the execution of his
duty and appealed.

HELD: (DC) It is the duty of a police officer to prevent
breaches of the peace which he reasonably apprehends. The
appellant was therefore guilty of obstructing the officer in the
execution of his duty. [1936] 1 K.B. 218

COMMENTARY
Lord Hewart C.J. considered that "the somewhat unsatisfactory case of *Beatty v. Gillbanks*" was not in point. However,
the speaker was here arrested not because of her conduct
but because the police feared possible violence from the
audience.

KEY PRINCIPLE: *Magistrates have common law powers to
bind persons over to keep the peace when there is reasonable
apprehension of a future breach of the peace.*

Lansbury v. Riley

The appellant was a supporter of women's suffrage and the
court was satisfied that he had been inciting others to commit
breaches of the peace in the cause of women's suffrage and

intended to carry on doing so. He was bound over by the metropolitan magistrate and appealed.

HELD: (DC) The court could order him to enter into recognisances and to find sureties for his good behaviour or be imprisoned in default of doing so. It was not essential to the exercise of the court's jurisdiction to make such orders that the conduct of the defendant should have caused any individual person to go in bodily fear. [1913] 3 K.B. 229

---

12. FREEDOM OF EXPRESSION

Reg v. Secretary of State for the Home Department, ex p. Brind
(For facts see page 8.)

HELD: (HL) The European Convention on Human Rights was not part of English law. Though it might be resorted to in order to resolve ambiguity or uncertainty in the provisions of a statute, no such ambiguity existed here and there was no presumption that the Secretary of State had to apply the Broadcasting Act in accordance with the Convention. The appeal would be dismissed. [1991] 1 A.C. 696

COMMENTARY
This formal banning power is rarely exercised. More frequently a form of self imposed censorship is employed within the broadcasting hierarchy. The Board of Governors of the BBC is appointed by the Government. Under the Broadcsating Act 1990 the Independent Television Commision must set up a code to ensure impartiality in programmes.

Defamation

KEY PRINCIPLE: *A local authority or central government may not sue for defamation.*

Derbyshire County Council v. The Times Newspapers

(For facts see page 5.)

HELD: (HL) Uninhibited public criticism of an elected body was vital in a democracy. The threat of libel actions would inhibit legitimate criticism. It was contrary to the public interest for central or local government institutions to have any common law right to sue for libel. The action would be struck out. [1993] A.C. 534

COMMENTARY
The House held that in the field of freedom of speech there was no difference in principle between English law and Article 10 of the Convention.

Confidentiality

KEY PRINCIPLE: *The equitable doctrine of breach of confidence is independent of other legal rights.*

Duchess of Argyll v. Duke of Argyll

After eight years of marriage the Duke sued for divorce on grounds of the Duchess's adultery. The marriage was dissolved in 1963. The Duchess published articles in a Sunday newspaper which included details of the Duke's personal conduct and financial affairs. The following year she sought interlocutory injunctions to restrain the Duke from giving to "*The People*" newspaper details of her private life, personal affairs or private conduct communicated to the Duke during the marriage.

HELD: (Ch D) A contract of confidence could be implied and a breach of contract or trust or faith could arise independently of any right of property. The court would act to restrain a breach of confidence independently of any right at law. Communication between husband and wife would be protected against breach of confidence. The Duchess's adultery did not entitle the Duke to publish the confidences of their married life. [1967] Ch. 302

COMMENTARY
An action based on breach of confidence was here extended to domestic secrets. In *Coco v. AN Clarke Ltd* (1969) R.P.C. 41 Megarry K.J. had set out the requirements for such an action as:

1. The information itself must "have the necessary quality of confidence about it".
2. The information must have been imparted in circumstances importing an obligation of confidence.
3. There must be an unauthorised use of that information to the detriment of the party communicating it. The following cases show the extension of these principles to other areas. This judgment illustrates that although there is no substantive law protecting privacy in Britain private confidences may be protected from publication.

Attorney General v. Jonathan Cape Ltd

(For facts, see page 2.)

HELD: (QB) The court had power to restrain publication in breach of confidence of information about the views of individual ministers expressed at Cabinet meetings, but there were no details of cabinet discussions in the diaries which required to be protected from publication. There was no ground in law which required the advice given by senior civil servants and ministerial observations on their capacities to remain confidential.

COMMENTARY

Lord Widgery C.J. said "I cannot see why the courts should be powerless to restrain the publication of public secrets, while enjoying the *Argyll* powers in regard to domestic secrets . . . in my judgment the Attorney General has made out his claim that the expression of individual opinions by Cabinet ministers in the course of Cabinet discussion are matters of confidence, the publication of which can be restrained by the court when this is clearly necessary in the public interest". However, he acknowledged that there must be a time limit after which the confidential character of the information and the duty of the court to restrain publication will lapse. The court should only intervene in the clearest of cases where the continuing confidentiality of the material has been demonstrated. This, ten years after the events described, was one of the less clear cases and restraint on publication was not appropriate.

KEY PRINCIPLE: *The degree of disclosure of confidential information must be justified in the public interest.*

Francome v. Mirror Group Newspapers

Unidentified persons tapped the telephone of a well-known jockey and made a recording said to show that he had broken the rules of racing. Two journalists from *The Daily Mirror* approached the jockey with the tapes to confirm their authenticity. The jockey and his wife obtained an injunction restraining publication of the tapes and ordering that the newspaper disclose their source. The judge ordered a speedy trial. The newspaper appealed against the injunction and the order to disclose.

HELD: (CA) It was not necessary in the interests of justice that the newspaper be forced to disclose its source since a speedy trial had been ordered. Publication of the tapes would prejudice the jockey's claim at trial and the injunction should be continued until trial, but its terms should be varied so that the newspaper could disclose the information obtained to the police or the jockey club. [1984] 1 W.L.R. 892

COMMENTARY

This case illustrates the attitude of the court to what is sometimes referred to as the iniquity defence. There may be a public interest in disclosing wrongful behaviour but this does not necessarily mean that this should be through the media. Limited publication to the police or some other authority, here the Jockey Club, may be appropriate. Another factor which Sir John Donaldson M.R. referred to in giving judgment was the claim by the editor of *The Daily Mirror* that it was expedient to break the law in obtaining the information. The editor accepted that publication would be an offence under section 5(b) of the Wireless and Telegraphy Act 1949. The occasions when the "moral imperative" required breaking a law would be extremely rare and "it was almost unheard of for compliance with the moral imperative to be in the financial or other best interests of the persons concerned".

KEY PRINCIPLE: *The court may apply equitable remedies to restrain unfair exploitation of a confidential fiduciary relationship.*

Schering Chemicals v. Falkman Ltd

Schering manufactured Primodos, a pregnancy-testing drug suspected of causing birth abnormalities. It was withdrawn from the market. The company hired Falkman Ltd to train its executives in presenting its point of view about the drug in public. In the course of the training sessions Schering revealed information in confidence to Falkman. Two actions by parents on behalf of affected children were begun. One of the instructors on the training course made a film with Thames television about the case. The film contained information which had been given in confidence, but which the instructor claimed was also available from publicly available sources. Schering obtained an injunction against publication. The defendants appealed.

HELD: (CA) Both Falkman Ltd and the instructor were under a fiduciary obligation to maintain the confidence placed in them. Thames television knew how the instructor had come by the information and so could not take advantage of his breach of duty. Lord Denning dissented on the basis that the public interest in knowing about Primodos outweighed the makers' private interest in preventing discussion of it. [1982] 1 Q.B. 1

COMMENTARY

This majority judgment has been much criticised. It could be argued that it gives more weight to business confidences than media freedom and is a controversial example of prior restraint. Lord Denning said that the press is not to be restrained in advance from publishing whatever it thinks right to publish. But the majority view was "The law of England is indeed as Blackstone declared a law of liberty; but the freedoms it recognises do not include a licence for the mercenary betrayal of business confidences".

KEY PRINCIPLE: *An interim injunction may be made to restrain publication in the interests of national security.*

Attorney-General v. The Guardian Newspapers Ltd

A former MI5 employee, Peter Wright, wrote *Spycatcher*, detailing unlawful activities carried out by the security services. Confidentiality clauses in his contract prevented publication in the United Kingdom but it was published in the United States. *The Observer* and *The Guardian* published an outline of his

allegations and were restrained by injunction from further
publication. The newspapers' appeal against the injunction
was dismissed. *The Independent* then published large extracts,
and two London evening papers published parts of what had
appeared in *The Independent*. *The Guardian* and *The Observer* then
sought to vary the injunction against them on the basis that
circumstances had changed. The Vice-Chancellor held that *The
Independent* and the two London evening papers were not in
contempt because they were not restrained by any injunction.
The Sunday Times then published extracts timed to coincide with
the U.S. publication of *Spycatcher*. The Court of Appeal reversed
the decision that *The Independent* was not in contempt and the
Attorney-General obtained an injunction against *The Sunday
Times*. The Court of Appeal allowed the newspapers to publish
a general summary of Wright's material. All the parties
appealed.

HELD: (HL) The injunction should be continued until the
hearing of the Attorney-General's action against *The Guardian*
and *The Observer* since to allow publication would deprive the
Attorney-General of the opportunity of having the matter
decided at trial. The court had a duty to prevent harm to
the security service and uphold its secrecy and to ensure that
court orders were not flouted. [1987] 1 W.L.R. 1248

COMMENTARY
This majority decision restored the original interlocutory
injunctions without the exception permitting *inter alia* reporting
of what had taken place in open court in the Australian proceedings. Government claims of the threat to national security
impelled the decision to maintain the injunctions despite the
massive publicity the book had received in the United States
and elsewhere. In a subsequent decision the House of Lords
confirmed that a third party although not named in an injunction restraining another newspaper from publishing confidential information was guilty of contempt if it nullified the purpose
of the original proceedings by destroying the confidentiality of
the information by publishing it (see *Attorney-General v. The
Times newspapers* (1991) at page 148).

KEY PRINCIPLE: *The government is only permitted to
restrain a breach of confidence if it can demonstrate that it*

is in the public interest to do so. It is entitled to profits from publications in breach of confidence.

Attorney-General v. The Observer Ltd

(sub nom. Attorney-General v. The Guardian Newspapers (No. 2))
The Attorney-General's action against *The Guardian* and *The Observer* came before Scott J. who held that Wright had broken his duty not to disclose information he had obtained while employed by MI5 but that *The Guardian* and *The Observer* were not in breach of their duty of confidentiality in publishing the articles they had published. *The Sunday Times* had been in breach of duty in publishing the first extract from the book, but secrecy had been destroyed by publication abroad of *Spycatcher* so the Attorney-General was not entitled to further injunctions, though *The Sunday Times* was liable to account for profits to the Attorney-General. The Court of Appeal dismissed appeals by the Attorney-General and *The Sunday Times*. Both appealed.

HELD: (HL) A duty of confidence could arise in contract or in equity. A third party with information known to be confidential was bound by a duty of confidence unless the material became generally known or there was a public interest in publication which outweighed the duty of confidence. The Crown could not show publication would be damaging since the confidential material had been published abroad. The Crown was entitled to profits for publication in breach of the injunction but not for future serialisation by *The Sunday Times*. [1990] 1 A.C. 109

COMMENTARY

This case marked the end of the long *Spycatcher* saga in the English courts, the trial on whether the injunctions should be permanent. In his speech Lord Goff saw no inconsistency between English law on this subject and Article 10 of the European Convention on Human Rights. He saw it as his obligation when he was free to do so "to interpret the law in accordance with the obligations of the Crown under this Treaty". He continued:

"The exercise of the right to freedom of expression under article 10 may be subject to restrictions (as are prescribed by law and are necessary in a democratic society) in relation to certain prescribed matters, which include 'the interests of national security' and 'preventing the disclosure of information received in confidence'. It is established in the jurisprudence of the European Court of Human Rights that the word 'necessary' in this context implies the existence of a pressing social need and that interference with the freedom of expression should be no more than is proportionate to the legitimate aim pursued. I have no reason to believe that English law as applied in the courts leads to any different conclusion."

In the event in *The Observer and The Guardian v. United Kingdom, The Sunday Times v. United Kingdom* [1991] 14 E.H.R.R. 153 the European Court of Human Rights considered that under the Convention the injunctions were necessary before publication of *Spycatcher* in the United States but not afterwards.

Contempt of Court

Contempt of Court Act 1981 (CCA)

KEY PRINCIPLE: *section 2(2): The strict liability rule applies only to a publication which creates a substantial risk that the course of justice in the proceedings in question with be seriously impeded or prejudiced.*

section 5: A publication made as or as part of a discussion in good faith of public affairs or other matters of general public interest is not to be treated as a contempt of court under the strict liability rule if the risk of impediment or prejudice to particular legal proceedings is merely incidental to the discussion.

KEY PRINCIPLE: *The word substantial in section 2(2) serves only to exclude remote risks, and serious impediment or prejudice refers to the consequences of publication. The burden of proof is on the prosecution to show section 5 did not apply and the test for the application of section 5 is (1) Is the publication a discussion? (2) was the risk of prejudice merely an incidental consequence of the publication?*

Attorney-General v. English

A consultant paediatrician was on trial for the murder of a Downs syndrome baby. The basis of the charge was an allegation that with the parents' approval he had allowed the baby to starve to death. During the trial, *The Daily Mail* published an article in support of a "Pro-Life" candidate at a by-election. The article said the candidate had been born without arms, but her chances of survival today were slight because she would probably be allowed to starve to death. The Divisional Court upheld an application by the Attorney-General for an order that the newspaper was in contempt of court. The newspaper appealed.

HELD: (HL) The article suggested that it was a common practice among paediatricians to do what was charged against the defendant, so the risk of prejudice was not remote and section 2(2) was satisfied. The newspaper was entitled to the protection of section 5 of the Contempt of Court Act 1981 because publication was made as part of a discussion of a matter of general public interest. It was for the Attorney-General to prove that a publication did not fall within section 5 and that the risk of prejudice to a fair trial was not "merely incidental" to the discussion. Section 5 was not merely an exception to the strict liability rule in section 2 of the 1981 Act, but stood on an equal footing with it and stated what publications should not amount to a contempt of court despite their tendency to interfere with the course of justice in particular proceedings. [1983] 1 A.C. 116

COMMENTARY
The court here seemed to be combining a liberal interpretation of section 2(2) with setting rather high standards for the prosecution to discharge under section 5. The interpretation of section 5 leaves the possibility that it cannot be applied to those articles which are aimed at exposing the behaviour of a particular individual because any prejudice will be a direct result of the main theme of the article rather than being an incidental effect of a discussion of matters of general public interest.

KEY PRINCIPLE: *In relation to Contempt of Court Act section 1 and section 2 there had to be a practical not a theoretical, substantial risk that the course of justice would be seriously impeded or prejudiced.*

Attorney-General v. The Guardian Newspapers
The judge in a fraud trial imposed reporting restrictions until other pending criminal proceedings against the defendants

were complete. The newspaper published an article under the heading "In big fraud trials, judges appear to be over-sensitive". On an application from the defence, the judge discharged the jury because the article might have affected the fairness of the trial. The Attorney-General brought committal proceedings against the newspaper for contempt of court.

HELD: (DC) The court was not convinced that in the circumstances the article had created a substantial practical risk that the course of justice would be seriously impeded or prejudiced. The publication was made as a discussion in good faith of a matter of general public interest to which the risk of prejudice to the proceedings was merely incidental. [1992] 1 W.L.R. 874

COMMENTARY

On delay before trial see *Attorney-General v. News Group newspapers.* [1987] Q.B. 1

KEY PRINCIPLE: *section 10 CCA: No court may require a person to disclose, nor is any person guilty of contempt of court for refusing to disclose, the source of information contained in a publication for which he is responsible, unless it be established to the satisfaction of the court that disclosure is necessary in the interests of justice or national security or for the prevention of disorder or crime.*

KEY PRINCIPLE:
1. a publisher could rely on section 10 even when an owner made a proprietary claim for the return of property; and
2. the onus of proving the matter fell on the party seeking disclosure.

Secretary of State for Defence v. The Guardian Newspapers Ltd

The newspaper obtained a leaked copy of a secret government memorandum on the handling of publicity about the installation of nuclear weapons at an airbase. The Secretary of State sought the return of the leaked document so that it could identify the informant. The newspaper resisted on the basis that it was protected by section 10 of the Contempt of Court Act 1981.

HELD: (HL) Section 10 applied if the order for disclosure might force the newspaper to reveal a source of information.

The publisher was not precluded from relying on section 10 in the face of a proprietary claim by the owner for the delivering up of his property. It was for the party seeking the order to prove on the balance of probabilities that the case fell within one of the four exceptions specified in section 10. The Crown had proved that disclosure was necessary in the interests of national security because whoever leaked it might in future leak other classified documents. [1985] A.C. 339

X v. Morgan Grampian Ltd

Bill Goodwin, a journalist on *The Engineer*, received from a source whose identity he agreed not to disclose a document about the financial affairs of two private companies. The companies obtained an injunction against publication and an order that the journalist disclose the source. He refused to comply with the order. He also refused to comply when the Court of Appeal varied the order to allow him to place the required information in a sealed envelope lodged with the court. He was found guilty of contempt and was refused a hearing at the Court of Appeal because of his refusal to comply with the order. The publishers and the journalist appealed.

HELD: (HL) The Court of Appeal had erred in refusing to hear the journalist, since the plaintiffs did not oppose his being heard and his appeal was based on an alleged lack of jurisdiction of the court to make the order. The court had power to order disclosure notwithstanding that the plaintiff's object in seeking it was to identify the source. The potential damage to the companies' business was great and there was no public interest in publication. [1991] 1 A.C. 1

COMMENTARY

Lord Bridge here disagreed with Lord Diplock's view in *Secretary of State for Defence v. The Guardian* (1984) (see page 142) in confining the meaning of "justice" in the section to "the technical sense of the administration of justice in the course of legal proceedings in a court of law". He said "It is in my opinion 'in the interests of justice' in the sense in which this phrase is used in section 10 that persons should be enabled to exercise important legal rights and to protect themselves from serious legal wrongs whether or not resort to legal proceedings in a court of law will be necessary to attain these objectives". However, this broad interpretation of the meaning of "interests of justice" in section 10 was limited in the judgment by the nature of the balancing exercise to be carried out. Disclosure will only be necessary in the interests of justice if such an interest is greater than the interest in protecting the source. One factor which weighed heavily here was the manner in which the information was obtained. Illegality in this connection will lessen the importance of protecting the source. In *Goodwin v. United Kingdom The Times*, March 28, 1996 the European Court of Human Rights held that the order to disclose the source was a violation of Article 10.

KEY PRINCIPLE: *The possibility that a professional judge or an appellate court would be influenced by any publication concerning cases they had to decide is remote.*

Re Lonrho Plc

Lonrho began judicial review proceedings in relation to the decision by the Secretary of State for Trade and Industry not to publish a report on the acquisition of House of Fraser by the Al Fayed brothers. While an appeal was pending in the proceedings, Tiny Rowland, Lonrho's chief executive, published a leaked copy of the report in *The Observer* which he owned. The Secretary of State obtained an injunction too late to prevent widespread distribution, and 3,000 copies were posted to various recipients, including to four of the Law Lords due to hear the appeal. The Secretary of State claimed that this was contempt of the House of Lords.

HELD: (HL) Only the House of Lords could decide whether there was a contempt. There was no risk that the course of justice would be impeded by the publication. It would be an extension of the law of contempt to hold that direct action by a litigant to secure the substance of a remedy which he was seeking in judicial proceedings amounted to a contempt of those proceedings. [1990] 2 A.C. 154

COMMENTARY

The decision makes it unlikely that publication of any material concerning a case before an appellate court or a judge in a civil trial without jury will be treated as contempt on the grounds that it is likely to prejudice the course of justice.

KEY PRINCIPLE: *Contempt of Court Act, s. 8: (1) Subject to subsection (2) below, it is a contempt of court to obtain, disclose or solicit any particulars of statements made, opinions expressed, arguments advanced or votes cast by members of a jury in the course of their deliberations in any legal proceedings. (2) This section does not apply to any disclosure of any particulars—(a) in the proceedings in question for the purpose of enabling the jury to arrive at their verdict, or in connection with the delivery of that verdict, or (b) in evidence in any subsequent proceedings for an offence alleged to have been committed in relation to the jury in the first mentioned proceedings, or to the publication of any particulars so disclosed.*

KEY PRINCIPLE: *A party may be liable under this section for disclosing information even where it was actually obtained by a third party.*

Attorney-General v. Associated Newspapers Ltd

The Mail on Sunday revealed what had happened in the jury room during a criminal trial, with accounts by three of the jurors as to how they had reached their decisions. The Attorney-General brought contempt proceedings against the newspaper under section 8(1) of the Contempt of Court Act 198, prohibiting disclosure of jury deliberations. The judge found contempt and the newspaper appealed.

HELD: (HL) The Act was intended to prevent publication of jury deliberations as well as their disclosure by individual jurors and the newspaper had been in contempt. The word "disclose" in the Act covered publication by a newspaper as well as disclosure by the jurors themselves. [1994] 2 A.C. 238

COMMENTARY

This section was brought in after *The New Statesman* was acquitted of contempt for publishing an interview with one of the jurors in the Jeremy Thorpe trial which revealed how the jury had reacted to certain witnesses. It revealed that the credibility of Peter Bessell, the chief prosecution witness, had been greatly damaged by his arrangement with *The Sunday Telegraph* that the fee for his story would be higher if there was a conviction. Contempt proceedings were not brought against *The Sunday Telegraph*. The new clause was brought in to stem what was thought to be a threat of cheque book journalism. It also has the disadvantageous effect of making research into jury decision-making more difficult.

Common Law Contempt

Contempt of Court Act, s. 6: Nothing in the foregoing provisions of this Act: (a) prejudices any defence available at common law to a charge of contempt of court under the strict liability rule; (b) implies that any publication is punishable as contempt of court under that rule which would not be so punishable apart from those provisions; (c) restricts liability for contempt of court in respect of conduct intended to impede or prejudice the administration of justice.

KEY PRINCIPLE: *Common law contempt of court includes deliberate or accidental interference with the outcome of particular judicial proceedings.*

Attorney-General v. The Times Newspapers

Distillers Ltd manufactured the drug Thalidomide which led to the birth of deformed children when taken in pregnancy by their mothers. The company was sued by victims and there were negotiations on a settlement of their claims. *The Sunday Times* published an article drawing attention to the plight of Thalidomide children. The company complained that the article was a contempt of court because litigation was still pending. The Divisional Court granted an injunction against further publication on the Attorney-General's motion. The matter was then raised in Parliament and there was a national campaign directed to putting pressure for a better deal for the victims. The Court of Appeal discharged the injunction. The Attorney-General appealed.

HELD: (HL) It was contempt of court to publish material which prejudged the issue of pending litigation. The article, which charged the company with negligence, was a contempt because negligence was one of the issues in the litigation. But temperate comment might have been permissible on the questions whether the legal remedies available were adequate and whether too much time had been taken up in legal proceedings. [1974] A.C. 273

COMMENTARY
The case was referred to the European Court of Human Rights and its judgment, holding that there had been a violation of Article 10 of the Convention led to the passing of the Contempt of Court Act 1981.

KEY PRINCIPLE: *Interfering with the administration of justice may constitute common law contempt even though no particular proceedings are at risk.*

R. v. The Socialist Worker Printers and Publishers Ltd, ex p. Attorney-General

During a blackmail trial at the Old Bailey the judge directed that the two victims of the alleged blackmail be referred to as Mr Y and Mr Z. Both gave evidence for the prosecution. Before the end of the trial, *The Socialist Worker* published an article by Paul Foot which gave the names and other details of the two men. The Attorney-General brought proceedings for contempt.

HELD: (QB) It was unlikely that the minds of the jury would have been influenced by the article, but its publication during the trial was an affront to the authority of the court and the publishers were in contempt. [1975] 1 Q.B. 635

COMMENTARY
At common law there is a power to order that witnesses be given anonymity in the wider interests of the criminal and civil process, quite apart from the need to do justice to the parties in any particular case. The rationale behind the finding here was that the publication was an affront to the court's authority and likely to inhibit blackmail victims from coming forward in the future.

KEY PRINCIPLE: *Orders as to publication may bind third parties if they know of the order and have the requisite mens rea.*

Attorney-General v. The Times Newspapers Ltd

Following the publication in various newspapers of extracts from Peter Wright's book *Spycatcher* (see *Attorney-General v. The Guardian Newspapers Ltd* and *Attorney-General v. The Observer Ltd* above) the Attorney-General brought committal proceedings for contempt of court against *The Sunday Times* and *The Independent*. Fines of £50,000 were imposed by Morritt J. and upheld on appeal. *The Sunday Times* appealed on the grounds that although the *mens rea* of contempt was present, the newspaper's conduct did not constitute the *actus reus* of contempt.

HELD: (HL) The injunction against publication of *Spycatcher* material had been granted pending trial of breach of confidence actions. The newspapers' actions had partly nullified the purpose of that trial and their conduct had impeded or interfered with the administration of justice, which was the *actus reus* of contempt. [1992] 1 A.C. 191

COMMENTARY
The case marked a controversial inroad into general principle of justice that a court order should only affect the party to which it is directed so that it can answer the case.

The case also underlines the necessity for *mens rea* in cases of contempt at common law. The parties had here conceded *mens rea*. At an earlier hearing the Court of Appeal had made it clear that the *mens rea* for common law contempt is specific intent and cannot include recklessness. The test is did the defendant either wish to prejudice proceedings or foresee that such prejudice was a virtually inevitable consequence of publication. Intentional contempt was a possible but not necessary inference if a person knows of an injunction and publishes anyway. Here the editors did not wish to interfere with the administration of justice but that did not preclude contempt. For a full discussion of *mens rea* see *Attorney-General v. News Group Newspapers Plc* page 149.

KEY PRINCIPLE: *Common law contempt may exist alongside statutory contempt.*

Attorney General v. Hislop

The Attorney-General sought to commit the editor of *Private Eye* for contempt of court. The proceedings related to articles published in February 1989 concerning the wife of the Yorkshire Ripper, while a previous libel action was pending. The application was dismissed on the grounds that the proceedings were unlikely to be prejudiced. The Attorney-General appealed.

HELD: The articles went beyond reasonable criticism. There was an intent to pervert the course of justice by trying to deter the Ripper's wife from pursuing her action and there was both common law and statutory contempt under the 1981 Act. Jurors might have read and been influenced by the articles. Appeal allowed. [1991] 1 Q.B. 514

COMMENTARY

The *actus reus* of common law contempt is making a publication which creates a real risk of prejudice to the admnistration of justice (see *Attorney-General v. Thompson Newspapers* [1968] 1 W.L.R. 1. In *Attorney-General v. The Times Newspaper* (above, page 148) the *actus reus* of contempt lay in one newspaper publishing despite a court order against another. In *Hislop* it lay in the threat to create prejudice in the jury.

KEY PRINCIPLE: *The* mens rea *of contempt is specific intention. Recklessness is not sufficient common law.*

Attorney-General v. News Group Newspapers Plc

The family of an eight-year-old girl alleged that she had been raped by a doctor. Police investigated but it was concluded there was insufficient evidence to justify prosecution. *The Sun* newspaper published details of the case and organised support for a private prosecution, which was brought in the Crown Court by the child's mother. The Attorney-General brought proceedings against the newspaper for contempt at common law.

HELD: (DC) The newspaper had shown the necessary intention to prejudice a fair trial by bringing to the attention of potential jurors damaging matters affecting the doctor which would be inadmissible in criminal proceedings. There could be common law contempt even though there were no pending or imminent proceedings. The newspaper's conduct in publishing the articles at the same time as encouraging and supporting a private prosecution was sufficient to constitute a common law contempt. [1989] 1 Q.B. 111

KEY PRINCIPLE: *Proceedings need not be active for common law contempt.*

Attorney-General v. The Sport Newspapers Ltd

After the disappearance of a schoolgirl in North Wales a local man with previous convictions for rape suddenly left the area. The police sought public help in tracing him but warned newspapers against publishing details of his previous convictions. *The Sport* newspaper published the details of his convictions. Two days later a warrant was issued for the man's arrest. The Attorney-General brought committal proceedings.

HELD: (DC) At the time of publication, there were no "active" proceedings, so the newspaper could only be guilty of contempt at common law. Common law contempt required specific intent to cause a real risk of prejudice to the due administration of justice. No such intent had been shown, so the newspaper had not been guilty of common law contempt. The court was divided over whether there could be contempt of imminent proceedings. [1991] 1 W.L.R. 1194

COMMENTARY
The law is in some doubt whether it is necessary to establish imminence. In *Attorney-General v. News Group Newspapers Plc* (see page 149) proceedings could not have been regarded as imminent but the court held *obiter* that where a publication was intended to interfere with justice and created a real risk of prejudice to proceedings contempt proceedings could be taken notwithstanding proceedings were neither pending nor imminent. The court was divided on this point in this case. Hodgson J. held contempt could not be committed at common law in relation to proceedings not yet in existence even if they were imminent. Bingham L.J. however held that a publication

made with the intention of prejudicing proceedings which although not in existence, are imminent, may be contemptuous. The matter is yet to be decided.

KEY PRINCIPLE: *Libel can be criminal if it is sufficiently serious.*

Criminal Libel

Gleaves v. Deakin

A private prosecution for criminal libel was brought against the author and publishers of a book. At the committal hearing the appellants sought to call evidence of the prosecutor's bad general reputation. The magistrate held he had no jurisdiction to admit the evidence and committed the case for trial. The Divisional Court refused applications for judicial review of the magistrate's decision. The defendants appealed.

HELD: (HL) Evidence of bad reputation of the prosecutor was not admissible at committal in proceedings for criminal libel, but had to await trial. The court felt that the law would be improved if criminal libel proceeds could be brought only with leave of the Attorney-General. [1980] A.C. 477

COMMENTARY
In the past criminal libel was used to prosecute political opponents of the government, such as John Wilkes and Tom Paine in the eighteenth century. Now there is widespread agreement that the offence should be abolished.

INDEX